# Reporting with Microsoft SQL Server 2012

Learn to quickly create reports in SSRS and Power View as well as understand the best use of each reporting tool

**James Serra**

**Bill Anton**

BIRMINGHAM - MUMBAI

# Reporting with Microsoft SQL Server 2012

Copyright © 2014 Packt Publishing

All rights reserved. No part of this book may be reproduced, stored in a retrieval system, or transmitted in any form or by any means, without the prior written permission of the publisher, except in the case of brief quotations embedded in critical articles or reviews.

Every effort has been made in the preparation of this book to ensure the accuracy of the information presented. However, the information contained in this book is sold without warranty, either express or implied. Neither the authors, nor Packt Publishing, and its dealers and distributors will be held liable for any damages caused or alleged to be caused directly or indirectly by this book.

Packt Publishing has endeavored to provide trademark information about all of the companies and products mentioned in this book by the appropriate use of capitals. However, Packt Publishing cannot guarantee the accuracy of this information.

First published: March 2014

Production Reference: 1100314

Published by Packt Publishing Ltd.
Livery Place
35 Livery Street
Birmingham B3 2PB, UK.

ISBN 978-1-78217-172-0

www.packtpub.com

Cover Image by Aniket Sawant (aniket_sawant_photography@hotmail.com)

# Credits

**Authors**
James Serra
Bill Anton

**Reviewers**
Paul Turley
Jen Underwood
Basit A. Masood-Al-Farooq
Varinder Sandhu

**Acquisition Editor**
James Jones

**Commissioning Editor**
Manasi Pandire

**Technical Editors**
Manan Badani
Shashank Desai

**Copy Editors**
Alisha Aranha
Sarang Chari

**Project Coordinator**
Aboli Ambardekar

**Proofreader**
Ameesha Green

**Indexer**
Rekha Nair

**Graphics**
Yuvraj Mannari

**Production Coordinator**
Shantanu Zagade

**Cover Work**
Shantanu Zagade

# About the Authors

**James Serra** is an independent consultant with the title Data Warehouse/Business Intelligence Architect. He is a Microsoft SQL Server MVP with over 25 years of IT experience. He started his career as a software developer, then was a DBA for 12 years, and for the last seven years, he has been working extensively with Business Intelligence using the SQL Server BI stack. At different times, he has been a permanent employee, consultant, contractor, and owner of his own business. All these experiences, along with continuous learning, have helped him to develop many successful data warehouse and BI projects. He is a noted blogger and speaker, having presented at the PASS Summit and the PASS Business Analytics conference. His blog is at JamesSerra.com.

He has earned the MSCE: SQL Server 2012 Business Intelligence, MSCE: SQL Server 2012 Data Platform, MCITP: SQL Server 2008 Business Intelligence Developer, MCITP: SQL Server 2008 Database Administrator, and MCITP: SQL Server 2008 Database. He has a Bachelor of Science degree in Computer Engineering from UNLV.

James resides in Houston, TX, with his wife Mary and three children: Lauren, RaeAnn, and James.

---

This book is dedicated to my wonderful wife Mary; my children Lauren, RaeAnn, and James; and my parents Jim and Lorraine. Their love, understanding, and support is what made this book possible. Now if they only understood the contents.

---

**Bill Anton** is an independent consultant whose primary focus is on designing and developing data warehouses and Business Intelligence solutions using the Microsoft BI stack. He has over 10 years of experience in the industry, and enjoys working closely with clients to overcome their data-related challenges. Bill is also an active member in the SQL Server community and enjoys sharing knowledge and helping others. When he's not working with the clients, he can usually be found answering questions on the MSDN forums, attending SQL PASS meetings, or writing blog posts at `http://byoBI.com`.

> I would like to thank my beautiful wife, Jena, for putting up with the long hours I've worked over the years. I would also like to thank James Serra, my mentor, for inviting me to contribute to this book and continuing to give me solid advice and perspective on the amazing industry in which we have the pleasure of working.

# About the Reviewers

**Paul Turley** is a mentor with SolidQ and a Microsoft SQL Server MVP. He consults, writes, speaks, and teaches Business Intelligence and reporting solutions. He works with companies around the world to visualize and deliver critical information to make informed business decisions. He is the lead author of *Professional SQL Server 2012 Reporting Services, Wrox Press*, a contributing author for *SQL Server Analysis Service 2012 Cube Development Cookbook, Packt Publishing*, and several other titles from Wrox and Microsoft Press. Paul blogs at `SqlServerBiBlog.com`.

**Jen Underwood** has almost 20 years of hands-on experience in the data warehousing, Business Intelligence, reporting, and predictive analytics industries. Prior to starting Impact Analytix, she held roles such as Microsoft Global Business Intelligence Technical Product Manager, Microsoft Enterprise Data Platform Specialist, Tableau Technology Evangelist, and also as a Business Intelligence Consultant for Big 4 Systems Integration firms. Through most of her career, she has been researching, designing, and implementing analytic solutions across a variety of open source, niche, and enterprise vendor landscapes, including Microsoft, Oracle, IBM, and SAP.

Recently, Jen was honored with a Boulder BI Brain Trust membership, a BeyeNetwork Prescriptive Analytics Channel, and a 2013 Tableau Zen Master (MVP) award. She also writes Business Intelligence articles for *SQL Server Pro* magazine.

Jen holds a Bachelor of Business Administration degree from the University of Wisconsin, Milwaukee, and a postgraduate certificate in Computer Science, Data Mining, from the University of California, San Diego.

**Basit A. Masood-Al-Farooq** is an internationally known Lead SQL DBA, trainer, and technical author, with twelve years of experience of the Microsoft technology stack. He is an accomplished development and production SQL Server DBA, with a proven record of delivering major projects on time and within budget. He is an expert at evaluating client needs against the capabilities of the SQL Server product set, with the objective of minimizing cost and maximizing function through making innovative use of advanced capabilities.

Basit has authored numerous SQL Server technical articles on various SQL Server topics for different SQL Server community sites that include `SQLMag.com`, `MSSQLTips.com`, `SQLServerCentral.com`, `SSWUG.org`, `SQL-SERVER-PERFORMANCE.com`, and `SearchSQLServer.com`. He has also developed and implemented many successful database infrastructures, data warehouse, and Business Intelligence projects. He also has a good understanding of ITIL principles.

He holds a Master's degree in Computer Science from London Metropolitan University and industry-standard certifications from Microsoft, Sun, Cisco, Brainbench, Prosoft, and APM, including MCITP Database Administrator 2008, MCITP Database Administrator 2005, MCDBA SQL Server 2000, and MCTS .NET Framework 2.0 Web Applications.

He can be reached via Twitter (`@BasitAali`), blog (`http://basitaalishan.com`), or via LinkedIn. (`http://uk.linkedin.com/in/basitfarooq`).

He has also reviewed *SQL Server 2012 Reporting Services Blueprints*, *Marlon Ribunal* and *Mickey Stuewe, Packt Publishing*.

---

I would like to thank my parents for getting me started on my journey, giving me the opportunity for a great education, allowing me to realize my own potential, and giving me the freedom to choose my career path. I am eternally grateful to my wife, Aniqa, and my sons, Rayyan and Saifaan, for giving me time to pursue a project like this and coping with my hectic work schedule.

---

**Varinder Sandhu** is an IT professional. He is a Microsoft Certified SQL Server – Database Administrator and Technology Specialist in Microsoft .NET Framework – Application Development Foundation. He holds a Master's degree in Computer Application (MCA) from Sikkim Manipal University and a Bachelor's degree in Computer Science from Guru Nanak Dev University, Amritsar. He has over six years of IT experience with contributions to all aspects of the software engineering process, from architecture and requirements definition, to designing, estimating, coding, testing, and maintaining software applications.

Last but not least, visit his blog at www.varindersandhu.in.

> I would like to thank my mom, dad, and my wife Gurpreet who always inspires me in my work.

# www.PacktPub.com

## Support files, eBooks, discount offers, and more

You might want to visit www.PacktPub.com for support files and downloads related to your book.

Did you know that Packt offers eBook versions of every book published, with PDF and ePub files available? You can upgrade to the eBook version at www.PacktPub.com and as a print book customer, you are entitled to a discount on the eBook copy. Get in touch with us at service@packtpub.com for more details.

At www.PacktPub.com, you can also read a collection of free technical articles, sign up for a range of free newsletters and receive exclusive discounts and offers on Packt books and eBooks.

http://PacktLib.PacktPub.com

Do you need instant solutions to your IT questions? PacktLib is Packt's online digital book library. Here, you can access, read and search across Packt's entire library of books.

### Why subscribe?

- Fully searchable across every book published by Packt
- Copy and paste, print and bookmark content
- On demand and accessible via web browser

### Free access for Packt account holders

If you have an account with Packt at www.PacktPub.com, you can use this to access PacktLib today and view nine entirely free books. Simply use your login credentials for immediate access.

### Instant updates on new Packt books

Get notified! Find out when new books are published by following @PacktEnterprise on Twitter, or the *Packt Enterprise* Facebook page.

# Table of Contents

| | |
|---|---|
| **Preface** | **1** |
| **Chapter 1: Getting Started with Reporting** | **5** |
|   **Standard reporting with SSRS** | **5** |
|   **Self-service reporting with Power View** | **8** |
|   **Power View limitations** | **9** |
|   **Reporting scenarios** | **10** |
|     Scenario 1 | 10 |
|     Scenario 2 | 11 |
|     Scenario 3 | 11 |
|     Scenario 4 | 11 |
|     Scenario 5 | 12 |
|     Scenario 6 | 12 |
|     Scenario 7 | 12 |
|     Scenario 8 | 13 |
|     Scenario 9 | 13 |
|     Scenario 10 | 13 |
|     Scenario 11 | 13 |
|     Scenario 12 | 14 |
|     Scenario 13 | 14 |
|   **Summary** | **14** |
| **Chapter 2: SSRS – Standard Reporting** | **15** |
|   **Primary components of a report** | **16** |
|     Data source | 16 |
|     Dataset | 18 |
|     Report items | 21 |
|   **Additional components of a report** | **28** |
|     Report parameters | 28 |
|     Expressions | 31 |

*Table of Contents*

| | |
|---|---|
| Actions | 32 |
| Custom code | 33 |
| **Report development environment** | **34** |
| **Server features and functionality** | **35** |
| Choosing an installation mode – SharePoint Integrated versus Native | 35 |
| Scheduling | 36 |
| Subscriptions | 37 |
| Report snapshots | 39 |
| Caching | 42 |
| Data alerts | 43 |
| My Reports (Native mode only) | 46 |
| Linked reports (Native mode only) | 47 |
| **Consuming reports** | **47** |
| Online | 47 |
| Offline | 48 |
| Data feed | 48 |
| Extensibility | 48 |
| Security | 49 |
| Roles and permissions | 49 |
| Securing Report Server objects | 50 |
| Data security | 51 |
| **Summary** | **52** |
| **Chapter 3: Development Activity with SSRS** | **53** |
| **Prerequisites** | **53** |
| **Tutorial scenario** | **54** |
| Creating a Reporting Services project | 54 |
| Creating a report object | 55 |
| Creating a shared data source | 56 |
| Adding reference to shared data source | 58 |
| Creating a dataset | 59 |
| Adding a report item | 61 |
| Deploying a report project | 66 |
| **Summary** | **68** |
| **Chapter 4: Power View – Self-service Reporting** | **69** |
| **Getting started** | **70** |
| **PowerPivot** | **72** |
| **Business Intelligence Semantic Model** | **73** |
| **Power View within SharePoint** | **74** |
| Setup | 74 |
| Tabular model connection | 75 |

[ ii ]

| | |
|---|---|
| Starting Power View connected to a tabular model connection | 77 |
| Multidimensional model connection | 78 |
| Starting Power View connected to a multidimensional model connection | 78 |
| **Power View within Excel 2013** | **79** |
| Setup | 79 |
| Data models | 79 |
| Starting Power View in Excel | 80 |
| Importing data into Excel | 80 |
| Adding data to a worksheet and inserting data into Power View | 81 |
| Not adding data to a worksheet and inserting data into Power View | 81 |
| Adding data to a worksheet and using PowerPivot | 82 |
| Not adding data to a worksheet and using PowerPivot | 82 |
| **Data visualizations** | **83** |
| **The user interface** | **84** |
| **Enhancing data models** | **88** |
| **Deploying and sharing reports** | **92** |
| **Presentation modes** | **93** |
| **Reports with multiple views in Power View** | **93** |
| Adding multiple views | 94 |
| Navigating among views | 94 |
| View filters | 94 |
| View preview images | 95 |
| **Chart highlighting, slicers, and filtering** | **95** |
| Chart highlighting | 95 |
| Slicers | 96 |
| Filtering | 98 |
| View-level/sheet-level filters | 98 |
| Visualization-level filters | 98 |
| Basic filters | 99 |
| Advanced filters | 100 |
| Search in filters | 101 |
| **Sorting** | **101** |
| **Export reports to Microsoft Office PowerPoint** | **102** |
| **Design tips** | **103** |
| Undo/Redo | 103 |
| Arranging visualizations | 103 |
| Fit to window | 103 |
| Pop out | 104 |
| **Summary** | **104** |

*Table of Contents*

| | |
|---|---|
| **Chapter 5: Development Activity with Power View** | **105** |
|   **Prerequisites** | **105** |
|   **Tutorial scenario** | **106** |
|     Creating a BI Semantic Model (BISM) connection | 106 |
|     Opening the Power View design interface | 108 |
|     Creating bar charts | 109 |
|     Creating pie charts | 111 |
|     Creating column charts | 113 |
|     Adding a slicer | 114 |
|     Deploying reports to SharePoint | 115 |
|   **Summary** | **117** |
| **Index** | **119** |

# Preface

Creating reports is natural in any business, and there are many Microsoft products for this purpose. However, the oldest and the most popular product is SQL Server Reporting Services (SSRS), which is ideal for any standard type of report. With technology evolving and the benefits of self-service reporting becoming evident, a new tool was needed. Microsoft responded to this need with Power View.

This book will cover all of the features of SSRS and Power View and will provide a step-by-step lab activity for each feature so that you can develop reports very quickly. You will learn the strengths and weaknesses of each tool, and thus be able to ascertain the best one to use for various reporting scenarios that you will encounter.

We, the authors of this book, are consultants who work with companies on a daily basis to design and create reports as well as help others to do so. When looking for a book to recommend to our clients that covers both SSRS and Power View, we found that books either talk about just one of these tools or include both but with limited information because they also cover a wide range of other reporting tools. Also, we could not find books that addressed the following topics: various reporting scenarios and the best tool to use for each; Power View for Excel 2013; the differences between Power View for SharePoint and Power View for Excel; and how SSRS is used for standard reporting, while Power View is used for self-service reporting. This book is our attempt to fill all these gaps.

## What this book covers

*Chapter 1, Getting Started with Reporting*, gives an introduction to SSRS and Power View and discusses which is the best tool to use in various reporting scenarios.

*Chapter 2, SSRS – Standard Reporting*, describes what standard reporting is and talks about how SSRS solves standard reporting needs, covering its main features and functionalities.

*Preface*

*Chapter 3*, *Development Activity with SSRS*, is a step-by-step lab activity that walks you through the process of creating a basic SSRS report.

*Chapter 4*, *Power View – Self-service Reporting*, describes what self-service reporting is and talks about how Power View solves self-service reporting needs, covering its main features and functionalities.

*Chapter 5*, *Development Activity with Power View*, is a step-by-step lab activity that walks you through the process of creating a basic Power View report.

# What you need for this book

To follow the step-by-step lab activities in this book, we recommend that you have a PC with the following software installed on it:

- Windows 7 or Windows 8
- Excel 2013
- SharePoint 2010 or SharePoint 2013
- SQL Server 2012 (the relational engine)
- SSRS 2012
- SQL Server Analysis Services 2012
- Power View
- SSDT or Visual Studio 2010

# Who this book is for

This book is intended for those who wish to learn the use of SSRS and Power View and need to understand the best use for each tool. This book will get you up and running quickly – no prior experience is needed with either of the tools!

# Conventions

In this book, you will find a number of styles of text that distinguish between different kinds of information. Here are some examples of these styles, and an explanation of their meaning.

Code words in text, database table names, folder names, filenames, file extensions, pathnames, dummy URLs, user input, and Twitter handles are shown as follows: "Regular users only have access to their own `My Reports` folder."

New terms and important words are shown in bold. Words that you see on the screen, in menus or dialog boxes for example, appear in the text like this: "One way to accomplish this is to use the **Windows Authentication** option for the credentials of the report data source(s)."

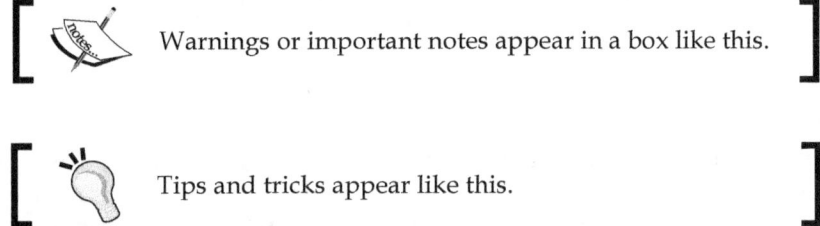

Warnings or important notes appear in a box like this.

Tips and tricks appear like this.

# Reader feedback

Feedback from our readers is always welcome. Let us know what you think about this book—what you liked or may have disliked. Reader feedback is important for us to develop titles that you really get the most out of.

To send us general feedback, simply send an e-mail to feedback@packtpub.com, and mention the book title via the subject of your message.

If there is a topic that you have expertise in and you are interested in either writing or contributing to a book, see our author guide on www.packtpub.com/authors.

# Customer support

Now that you are the proud owner of a Packt book, we have a number of things to help you to get the most from your purchase.

## Errata

Although we have taken every care to ensure the accuracy of our content, mistakes do happen. If you find a mistake in one of our books—maybe a mistake in the text or the code—we would be grateful if you would report this to us. By doing so, you can save other readers from frustration and help us improve subsequent versions of this book. If you find any errata, please report them by visiting http://www.packtpub.com/submit-errata, selecting your book, clicking on the **errata submission form** link, and entering the details of your errata. Once your errata are verified, your submission will be accepted and the errata will be uploaded on our website, or added to any list of existing errata, under the Errata section of that title. Any existing errata can be viewed by selecting your title from http://www.packtpub.com/support.

# Downloading the color images of the book

We also provide you a PDF file that has color images of the screenshots/diagrams used in this book. The color images will help you better understand the changes in the output. You can download this file from: https://www.packtpub.com/sites/default/files/downloads/1720EN_ColoredImages.pdf

# Piracy

Piracy of copyright material on the Internet is an ongoing problem across all media. At Packt, we take the protection of our copyright and licenses very seriously. If you come across any illegal copies of our works, in any form, on the Internet, please provide us with the location address or website name immediately so that we can pursue a remedy.

Please contact us at copyright@packtpub.com with a link to the suspected pirated material.

We appreciate your help in protecting our authors, and our ability to bring you valuable content.

# Questions

You can contact us at questions@packtpub.com if you are having a problem with any aspect of the book, and we will do our best to address it.

# 1
# Getting Started with Reporting

Every business needs reports and usually lots of different types of reports. In the Microsoft realm, there is not just one product that creates all of these reports. While having multiple tools gives you many advantages, it leads to confusion about which is the best tool to use for a specific task. There are numerous reporting tools, and we will talk about two of them: the oldest and most widely used—**SQL Server Reporting Services** (**SSRS**) and the new kid on the block—**Power View**. We will explain both of these tools so that you can quickly use them and have clarity on the best use of each tool.

## Standard reporting with SSRS

SSRS has been around for quite a long time. It was first released in 2004 as an add-on to SQL Server 2000. Over the years, it has seen many improvements, making it by far the most widely used Microsoft reporting tool.

Despite the multitude of new reporting tools with their fancy and cool features, there is still a huge demand for standard corporate reports, also called **canned reports** or **operational reports**, which SSRS is ideal for.

*Getting Started with Reporting*

SSRS is a feature-rich, flexible, and scalable reporting platform that can satisfy the needs of everyone from small businesses to fortune 500 companies. The following screenshot shows an SSRS report in the design mode using Visual Studio 2012:

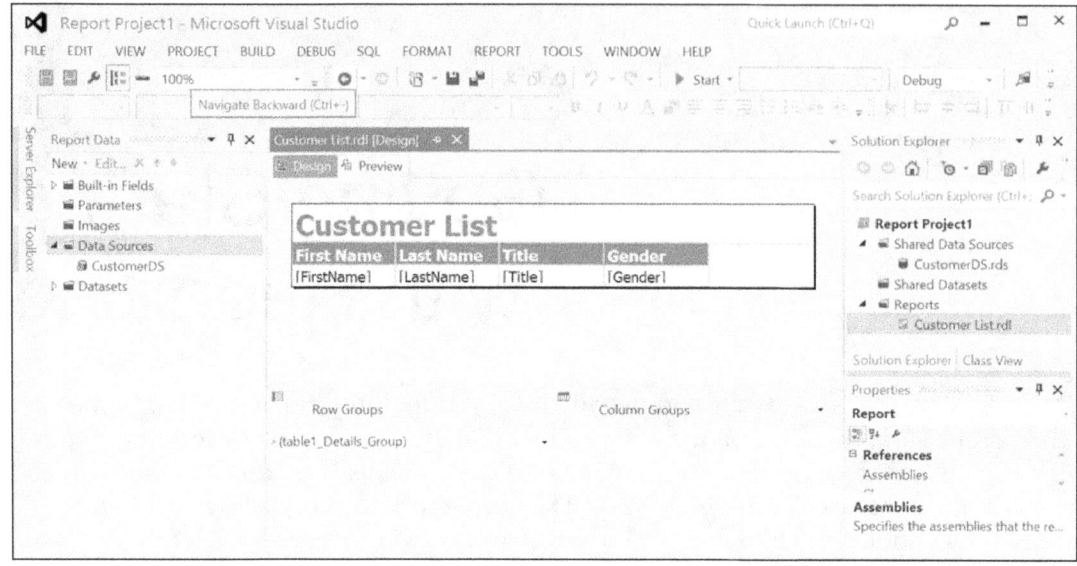

An SSRS project in Visual Studio 2012

SSRS supports dozens of data sources including SQL Server, SQL Azure, SSAS multidimensional models and tabular models, Parallel Data Warehouse, OLE DB, ODBC and, a SharePoint list. It is a powerful report-authoring and management environment that allows the creation of static and parameterized reports. The reports are built using Visual Studio or **SQL Server Data Tools for Business Intelligence (SSDT-BI)**, which provides a drag-and-drop interface as well as wizards that generate a **Report Definition Language (RDL)** file based on XML. This allows for most of the reports to be built without having to write any code.

There is also a simpler-to-use and more streamlined reporting tool called **Report Builder 3.0** that looks and feels more like an Office application than the project-centric development tool SSRS. It is a popular tool that also creates an RDL file that can be used by SSRS. Report Builder has about 80 percent of the features and capabilities of SSRS, so it is geared more toward a person who needs a very easy-to-use tool and is willing to sacrifice some flexibility (nevertheless, the RDL file created in Report Builder can always be opened in SSRS to add any missing functionality).

SSRS offers two modes of installation and operation: **Native mode** and **SharePoint Integrated mode**. Native mode provides a standalone report server called Report Manager, which offers report viewing, administration, security, processing, and delivery. SharePoint Integrated mode provides the report server through a SharePoint server and almost all the features that are present in Native mode. However, certain features, such as security and storage, are integrated within SharePoint. Most companies select SharePoint Integrated mode as it provides a unified portal to store and present all documents and reports.

The previously mentioned RDL files are uploaded to the Report Manager or the SharePoint document library. All the reports can be accessed through either of the portals and can be automatically generated and distributed. Users can perform analysis using parameters, filters, drill-down, and drill-through. Reports can be scheduled and distributed via the portal, a file share, e-mail, or a printer, and can be rendered as PDF, Excel, XML, comma delimited text file, various image types (TIFF, BMP, GIF, JPEG, EMF, PNG, WMF), HTML, or Microsoft Word formats. The following screenshot shows an output of an SSRS report in Report Manager:

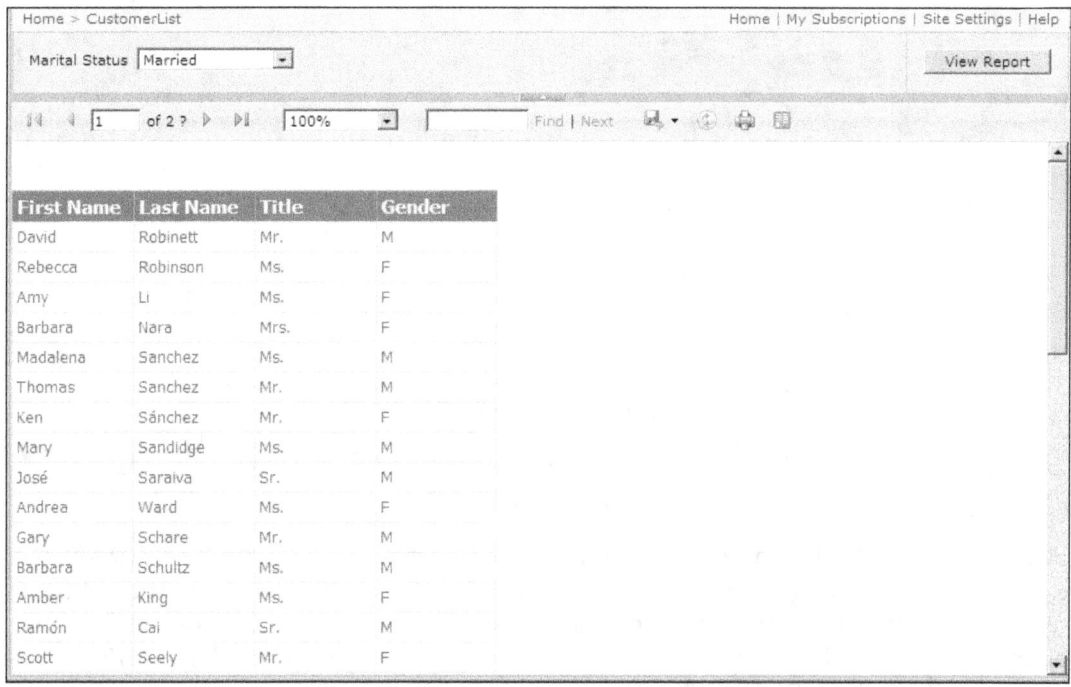

Running a report in Report Manager

# Self-service reporting with Power View

While SSRS is a great solution, companies frequently need to go beyond these static reports to visualize their data in different ways to help them make better business decisions. This is where Power View comes into the picture. Power View is an easy-to-use solution that allows users to quickly create highly-interactive and visual reports that can be accessed in a variety of different ways and from different devices. The reporting experience is greatly simplified as there are no setting properties on objects, no design mode, no creating of relationships with the data, and no connecting items together for filtering. The following screenshot shows a report being created in Power View:

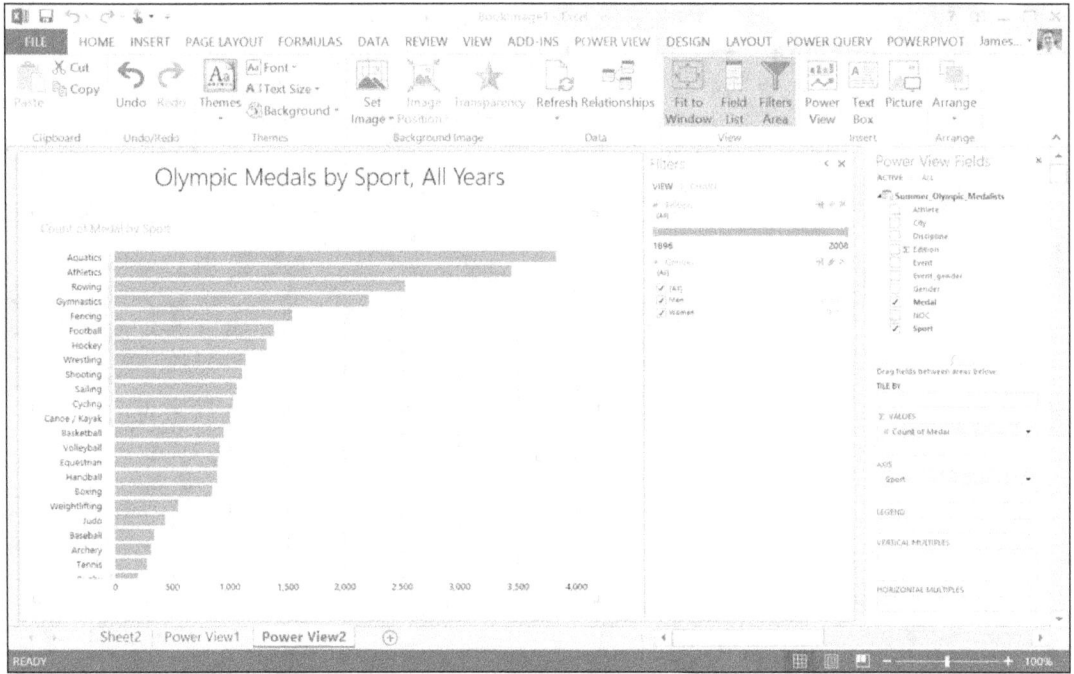

Creating a report in Power View

Introduced with SQL Server 2012 and integrated with the SharePoint Enterprise edition, Power View has become very popular due to its ease of use and the ability to generate very useful and cool looking reports. It was first available only through SharePoint Server (Enterprise edition), but now it is available as an Excel 2013 add-on in the Office 2013 ProPlus edition.

Power View in SharePoint can connect to Excel PowerPivot workbooks and SSAS multidimensional models and tabular models (also known as cubes). An Excel PowerPivot workbook can use many different data sources such as SQL Server, SQL Azure, text file, and Microsoft Access.

Power View in Excel 2013 uses as the basis of a report either an internal data model or an external data model such as another workbook or a **SQL Server Analysis Services** (**SSAS**) tabular model. Note that Power View in Excel 2013 does not support a multidimensional model. The internal data model can use many different data sources such as SQL Server, SQL Azure, text file, and Microsoft Access.

However, Power View is not a replacement for SSRS as both tools have their place: Reporting Services is an ideal solution for corporate reporting, and Power View is better suited for self-service reporting with established data models. Power View was developed by the Microsoft Reporting Services product team who saw it as part of the total SSRS offering.

Power View should be the tool of choice for self-service reporting for the following reasons:

- Power View is easier to use than Report Builder 3.0, which is Microsoft's other self-service tool. While Power View does not have all the features of Report Builder as yet, it is much quicker and simpler to use. On the other hand, there are a lot of features in Power View that are not in Report Builder.
- Because it is an Excel add-in, it allows for an easy transition from pulling in and modifying data in an Excel-hosted PowerPivot model to generating a report of that data in Power View.
- A Power View report can be embedded in PowerPoint (SharePoint 2010 or 2013 and Enterprise edition only). It's as simple as saving your Power View report as a PowerPoint presentation. You can even filter, slice, and explore your Power View report within PowerPoint if you have an active connection to the SharePoint server.
- It is very interactive with no design or preview mode, which you would otherwise have to switch between. The only mode it has is **What You See Is What You Get** (**WYSIWYG**). It is very easy to add fields, filters, and aggregations. Everything is done instantly thanks to the use of Silverlight.

## Power View limitations

While you will have some SSRS reports that can be replaced with Power View reports, be aware of its limitations that can prevent the replacement of other reports. The limitations are as follows:

- Power View does not have nearly as many customization options as SSRS. With SSRS, you can change just about every property of a report item, but Power View is very limited in terms of the properties you can change.

*Getting Started with Reporting*

- The current implementation of Power View requires the installation of a Silverlight browser plugin. This can add complications that you generally don't have with SSRS because it does not require any browser plugins. In addition, Silverlight is a dying technology and is being replaced with HTML 5 (Microsoft is working on a HTML 5 Power View client).
- Power View in SharePoint requires SharePoint Enterprise and the installation of Reporting Services in SharePoint Integrated mode. SSRS will work with the Standard edition of SharePoint and has a Native mode that does not require SharePoint. Power View also works with Excel 2013 (ProPlus edition only), but many companies have not yet upgraded to it and are still using Excel 2010. Additionally, if you are using Excel 2013, it is likely that you still want to use SharePoint Enterprise to share the reports instead of sharing the workbook.
- Power View does not support the passing of parameters, whereas SSRS does.
- Power View does not have any means of scheduling reports or automatic report delivery. On the other hand, SSRS has a sophisticated way of scheduling and delivering reports using subscriptions.
- Power View does not support custom code, so there is no way to extend its features. SSRS is very flexible in allowing you to extend its code, so you can do just about anything with it.

## Reporting scenarios

Which is the best reporting tool for the job? The following are various reporting scenarios you may encounter and our suggestions on the best tool to use along with the reasons why:

## Scenario 1

You want the reports to be created automatically and delivered via e-mail to certain users every morning. For such reports, you will pass in certain parameters such as country codes and the beginning and ending dates.

**Solution**: Since Power View does not support scheduled rendering and delivery of reports or parameter passing, SSRS is the reporting tool to use in this situation. In fact, this is what SSRS excels at thanks to the sophisticated subscription feature. This feature allows you to register with a publisher to get any report on a scheduled/reoccurring basis. A subscription includes parameters and a recipient list, rendering format, delivery schedule, and delivery method.

There are two types of subscriptions: standard subscription and data-driven subscription. With a standard subscription, report parameters are provided at the time of subscription and cannot be changed at runtime. A data-driven subscription allows parameter values to be returned from a query during the execution of the report.

## Scenario 2

You need to create a report but are not sure what you want it to look like. Also, you want to explore the data and build a report on the fly.

**Solution**: Power View is ideal for users who don't know up front how they will combine and analyze the data. Moreover, they don't know what question to ask. Instead, they want to discover the meaning in the data and slice and dice the data. Power View's main purpose is just that type of ad hoc situation, whereas SSRS requires you to have a clear idea of what the report should look like and what data should be used.

## Scenario 3

You need to create a simple report quickly.

**Solution**: While SSRS was originally created for technical users (developers), it has evolved into a more self-service tool for power business users. However, it still has a steep learning curve. On the other hand, Power View is very easy to use and extremely intuitive. Although you may sacrifice certain features by using Power View, you can generate a report very quickly, even if you have never used Power View before.

## Scenario 4

You want to generate a report that has a list of all the orders from the last week.

**Solution**: SSRS is the tool that you use when generating a report that contains details at the lowest grain, such as a list of orders or a customer list. Power View can generate details but is much more suited for viewing higher-level summaries of data.

## Scenario 5

You need to export your reports to Microsoft Word.

**Solution**: SSRS allows you to export to Microsoft Word, whereas Power View does not. Power View in Excel 2013 exports to PDF, Excel, XML, HTML, and comma delimited text file. In the SharePoint version of Power View, it can only export to PowerPoint. With SSRS, you can export to PDF, Excel, XML, comma delimited text file, TIFF image, HTML, and Microsoft Word formats.

## Scenario 6

You want to create a report where you can perform a drill-down and drill-through of various summaries of the data.

**Solution**: Drill-down allows you to go from a general view of the data to a more specific one at the click of a mouse (for example, going from the sales of a state to sales of the cities in that state). A drill-through action allows you to jump to another report that is relevant to the data being analyzed in the current report, also at the click of a mouse (that is, going from showing sales by state in a tabular form to sales by state in a country map). In SSRS, a drill-through requires manually creating a drill-through action in the main report and passing parameters to other reports, which you must create. For drill-down, you must manually define the groups and detail rows or columns and then hide them, which are then accessed with a plus sign that the user clicks on. However, these can be time-consuming tasks that require a lot of coding. In Power View, it is much easier: drill-down requires you to create a hierarchy and add it to a report or create a matrix report and enable drilling down on rows. There is no additional coding as drill-down support is performed automatically; drilling down is just a matter of double-clicking on the row or column you want to drill into. Drill-through is done in Power View by simply clicking on the various chart types in the **Switch Visualization** section of the design ribbon and the chart is automatically changed.

## Scenario 7

You need to do a lot of chart formatting for you report.

**Solution**: SSRS allows you to have finely detailed control over many of the individual elements in any chart you want to display. While in Power View, there is a very limited number of customization options. So while it is much quicker to build a chart in Power View than in SSRS, if you need a lot of customization for your chart, SSRS is the tool to use.

## Scenario 8

You need to create a map, display data on it, and create lot customizations for the map and the data.

**Solution**: SSRS and Power View both include mapping capabilities. But like the previous answer in which SSRS allows for more customization of charts than Power View, SSRS also allows for much greater customization of the maps. So if you need to create a map quickly and don't need much customization, go with Power View. But if you need a lot of customizations of the map, go with SSRS.

## Scenario 9

You want to create a report that animates the progression of data over time.

**Solution**: SSRS does not have an option that supports this, but Power View does. It accomplishes this through scatter and bubble charts. To view changes in data over time in Power View, add a time dimension to the scatter and bubble charts and a play axis. When you click on the play button, the bubbles travel, grow, and shrink to show how the values change based on the play axis.

## Scenario 10

You want to integrate the report with other custom applications.

**Solution**: SSRS is an open and extensible reporting platform that provides developers with a large set of APIs for developing solutions. There are three options when integrating SSRS into custom applications: the Report Server Web service (also known as the Reporting Services SOAP API), the ReportViewer control for Microsoft Visual Studio, and URL access. Power View has no such option for integrating the reports with applications, other than embedding a Power View report into an HTML frame. Moreover, there is little control over sizing and toolbar options.

## Scenario 11

You want to create a dashboard.

**Solution**: You can create dashboards in both products. With Power View, you can quickly create a very slick-looking dashboard that has a lot of visual impact; however, the customization of the dashboard is limited. With SSRS, there are more customizations when creating a dashboard, but the dashboards won't look nearly as slick as Power View, and it could take a lot of coding to obtain the same functionality that you have with Power View; this is especially the case if you want to have a lot of interactivity.

## Scenario 12

You want to create monthly management reports that are mostly static and want users to be able to subscribe to these reports.

**Solution**: SSRS is the perfect choice for this situation. It excels in allowing you to create mostly static reports, where you just have a few filtering options. Also, users can easily subscribe to any report and choose when and how they want the report delivered. On the other hand, Power View is geared more toward non-static, heavily interactive types of reports and does not have an option to subscribe to them.

## Scenario 13

Your manager wants you to dig into the data and find out why a particular store is underperforming. You are trying to answer a single, specific business question.

**Solution**: A typical scenario is that a manager sees a SSRS report that indicates a trouble spot, such as a store that is underperforming, based on some predefined threshold. The SSRS report has no ability to slice and dice the report to find out what is causing the store to underperform, so the manager asks you to try and find out why. This is where Power View comes into the picture. It's the perfect tool to pull in data for the underperforming store and slice and dice it to find out the underlying issue. Maybe when you dig into the details, you will find it's a particular product that is the problem and action can be taken to improve the sales of that one product.

## Summary

In this chapter, we learned the difference between standard reporting and self-service reporting and how SSRS is ideal for the former and Power View for the latter. We got a brief overview of these two products and the data sources they use, and discussed Power View's limitations, which prevent it from being the tool used for all reporting. Finally, we saw certain reporting scenarios and discussed the best tool to use and why.

In the next chapter, we will start using SSRS and cover it in more detail.

# 2
# SSRS – Standard Reporting

**SQL Server Reporting Services (SSRS)** is Microsoft's primary technology for delivering standard reports. As mentioned in the previous chapter, these types of reports typically contain a well-defined output that is known and developed by a member of the IT department ahead of time and delivered on a recurring basis to facilitate the regular daily, weekly, and even monthly decision-making needs of the business.

One of the great capabilities of SSRS is the fine-grained control it allows users over visualizations, layout, parameterization, and extensibility, providing for a level of customization that simply can't be matched by any other reporting tool in the Microsoft stack. In fact, it is this ability of control and customization that also makes SSRS well suited for the development and delivery of complex dashboards and scorecards, even though there are arguably more suitable tools (for example, PerformancePoint) for this purpose when requirements are more basic.

At the same time, such a great level of control comes with the cost of a higher-than-necessary development effort and, therefore, can often be viewed as an impediment to the delivery of information to the business. SSRS, despite having been marketed in the past as a self-service reporting tool via Report Builder, requires an IT skill set to develop all but the most basic reports. It is for this very reason that we have seen the rise of self-service reporting tools over the last few years.

In this chapter, we'll cover the main features and functionalities offered in SQL Server Reporting Services 2012, including a breakdown of report components, development experience, extensibility, and security. By the end of the chapter, readers should have an understanding of the capabilities offered in SQL Server Reporting Services.

# Primary components of a report

Before diving into all the cool features and functionalities offered by SSRS, it is important to have a basic understanding of the primary components that make up an SSRS report as well as a mental model of how these components work together to deliver information to the business; which is, after all, the entire purpose of standard reporting.

The primary components of an SSRS report are as follows:

- Data source
- Dataset
- Report item

The following diagram shows how data flows from the source system through these components and out to the end user:

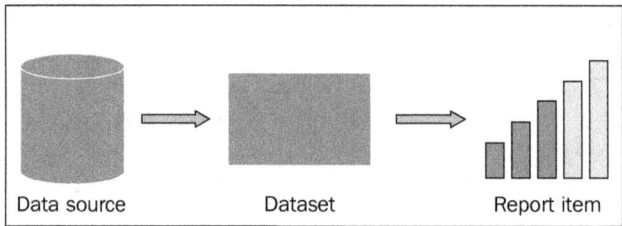

Flow of data through primary report components

## Data source

A data source is typically the first object created while building an SSRS report and contains all the information necessary to make a connection to a source system. The source system could be a SQL Server database, Analysis Services cube, a SharePoint list, or some other type of business application database such as Oracle.

While most reports typically pull data from a single data source, it is possible to pull data from multiple sources. In fact, a single report can be based on multiple data sources and multiple datasets. The following screenshot shows the full list of data sources that can be used with SSRS 2012 right out of the box:

Full list of available data sources

 Data sources use credentials to authenticate with the source system. Credentials can be stored with the data source or determined at runtime. Some Reporting Services features, such as subscriptions and snapshots, require a data source with stored credentials. We will cover credentials in more detail toward the end of this chapter in the section on security.

There are two types of data sources: shared and embedded. A shared data source exists as a standalone object outside of the SSRS report and can be reused and referenced by multiple SSRS reports. An embedded data source is specific to a single SSRS report. If you open an SSRS report file in a text editor, you can find a section (shown in the following screenshot) that contains the details of all the data sources included in the report. Notice that the snippet for the shared data source (`DataSource2`) only includes the information needed to locate the shared data source object on the report server, while the snippet for the embedded data source includes a connection properties section with all the information needed to connect to the source system.

```
<DataSources>
  <DataSource Name="DataSource1">
    <ConnectionProperties>
      <DataProvider>SQL</DataProvider>
      <ConnectString>Data Source=.;Initial Catalog=AdventureWorksDW2012</ConnectString>
      <IntegratedSecurity>true</IntegratedSecurity>
    </ConnectionProperties>
    <rd:SecurityType>Integrated</rd:SecurityType>
    <rd:DataSourceID>417eac9d-d1cc-4c10-b5f1-5b0a5ff5a6cb</rd:DataSourceID>
  </DataSource>
  <DataSource Name="DataSource2">
    <DataSourceReference>SharedDataSource1</DataSourceReference>
    <rd:SecurityType>None</rd:SecurityType>
    <rd:DataSourceID>4f1a7e12-3c76-4b2e-9197-f661296aa299</rd:DataSourceID>
  </DataSource>
</DataSources>
```

XML code of SSRS report showing references to embedded dataset (top) and shared dataset (bottom)

One of the main benefits of using a shared data source is that it makes managing changes easier. This is especially true for large organizations, where you may have hundreds of reports based on the same relational source system. Imagine the headache and effort required to update the connection details for all of those reports if the source system is migrated to a new server. However, there are certain scenarios where an embedded data source is the only option. One example where the data source must be embedded is when you want to use an expression to dynamically control the destination of a data source object. Expressions will be covered later in this chapter.

# Dataset

A dataset is best thought of as a two-dimensional table structure based on the results of a query that has been executed against a report data source such as that displayed in the following screenshot:

| Category | Calendar Year | Month of Year | Total Sales Amount | Total Product Cost | Total Profit |
|---|---|---|---|---|---|
| Accessories | CY 2007 | July | $14,468.20 | $5,411.13 | $9,057.07 |
| Accessories | CY 2007 | August | $52,056.61 | $19,469.26 | $32,587.35 |
| Accessories | CY 2007 | September | $52,149.72 | $19,504.08 | $32,645.64 |
| Accessories | CY 2007 | October | $54,595.17 | $20,418.68 | $34,176.49 |
| Accessories | CY 2007 | November | $54,832.02 | $20,507.27 | $34,324.75 |
| Accessories | CY 2007 | December | $65,607.99 | $24,537.50 | $41,070.49 |
| Accessories | CY 2008 | January | $56,456.93 | $21,114.99 | $35,341.94 |
| Accessories | CY 2008 | February | $56,995.90 | $21,316.57 | $35,679.33 |
| Accessories | CY 2008 | March | $60,097.80 | $22,476.68 | $37,621.12 |
| Accessories | CY 2008 | April | $62,673.58 | $23,440.03 | $39,233.55 |
| Accessories | CY 2008 | May | $71,880.47 | $26,883.41 | $44,997.06 |
| Accessories | CY 2008 | June | $65,200.93 | $24,385.26 | $40,815.67 |
| Accessories | CY 2008 | July | $33,744.64 | $12,620.55 | $21,124.09 |

Report dataset

This is not meant to imply that the results of the query are materialized in a physical structure, although that is an option if caching is configured.

>  Caching the result set of a query may seem wasteful. However, when viewed from a more holistic perspective, the benefits can be substantial. Given the nature of standard reporting—where the same reports are being run by large numbers of users—the ability to cache the data retrieved from the source system can provide considerable performance gains and greatly reduce the load placed on the source system. We'll cover this topic in more detail later in the chapter.

While creating a dataset, the developer first chooses the data source, which can be a shared data source referenced by the report or an embedded data source created and contained within the report. Once the data source has been selected, a query is created—the results of which will be made available as a two-dimensional structure—like the one in the preceding screenshot, which can then be consumed by the various report items.

It is important to understand that the use of the word "query" in the preceding paragraph is in the most general sense. The type of query is completely dependent on the data source. For example, if the data source is a relational database, the query could be a standard SQL select statement, or it could be the result set from a stored procedure. On the other hand, if the data source is an Analysis Services database, the query could be an MDX query (for a multidimensional cube), a DMX query (for a data mining model), or even a DAX query (for a tabular model that is new to SQL Server 2012).

Dataset queries can be entered manually as text or constructed using the graphical query designer shown in the following screenshot. The graphical query designer is helpful when the report author is not very familiar with the query language. However, report authors who are more proficient in the query language are likely to prefer the manual entry method or a combination of the two.

SSRS – Standard Reporting

>  Though not a requirement, when the data source is a relational database, it is considered good practice to use a stored procedure to retrieve data for the dataset instead of a query embedded in the report. This offers an additional layer of encapsulation that comes in handy if/when minor changes are required at a later point in time. There may also be potential performance benefits through query parameterization and planned cache reuse on the source system, although thorough testing is the only way to be sure.

The **Query Designer** window is as follows:

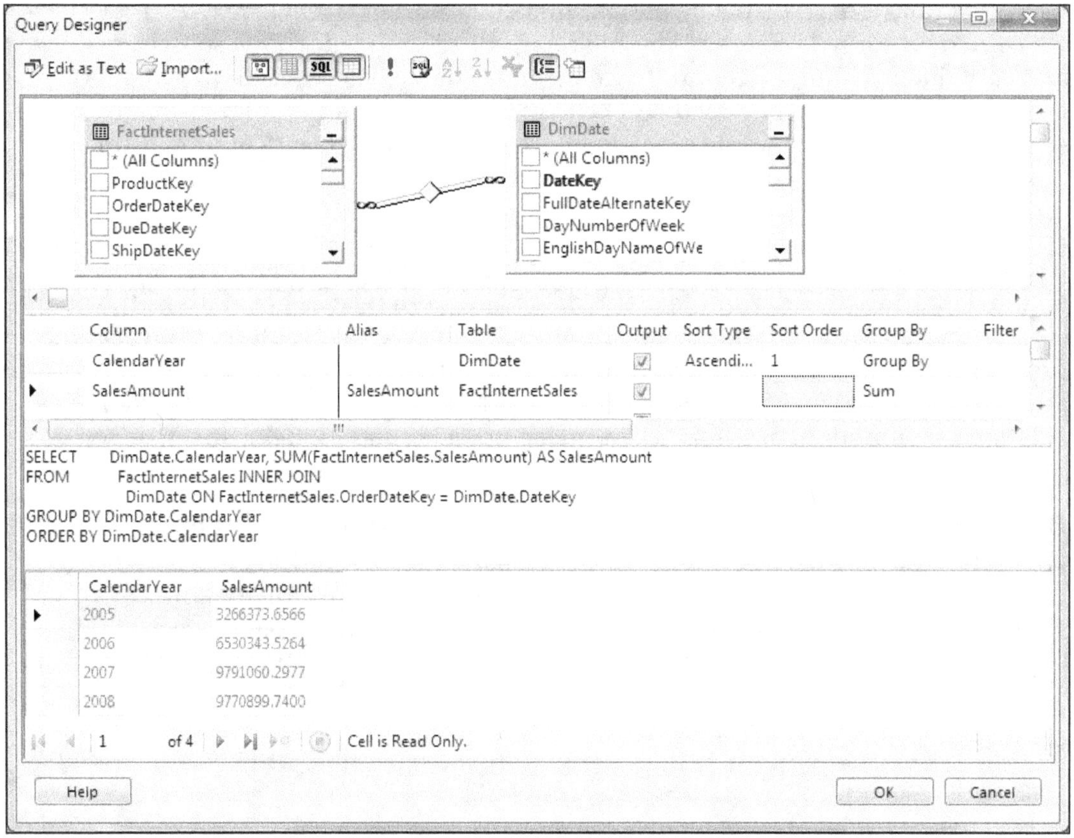

![Query Designer window screenshot]

Graphical query designer used to help construct SQL queries for datasets

Just as with the data source component, a dataset component can be shared or embedded. A shared dataset exists as a standalone object and can be referenced by multiple reports, while an embedded dataset is specific to a single report. A shared dataset cannot be based on an embedded data source; it must be based on a shared data source.

Datasets can be filtered to limit the data displayed on a report. However, it is typically better to push the filter down into the query defined in the dataset. This will maximize performance by only retrieving data from the source that needs to be displayed in the report. When the filter is applied to the dataset itself, all the data is retrieved from the data source and pulled into the dataset object, after which the filter is applied before data is consumed by the various report items.

## Report items

Report items refer to the visual items that are placed directly on the report (referred to as the report body during authoring) that display information to the user. A report item can be a table, chart, gauge, map, or any of a number of different items.

Just as a dataset is linked to a specific data source, a report item is linked to a specific dataset. Looking at it from the other direction, many report items can be linked to the same dataset just as many datasets can be linked to the same data source. The following diagram helps you to visualize the cascading one-to-many relationship between these primary report components:

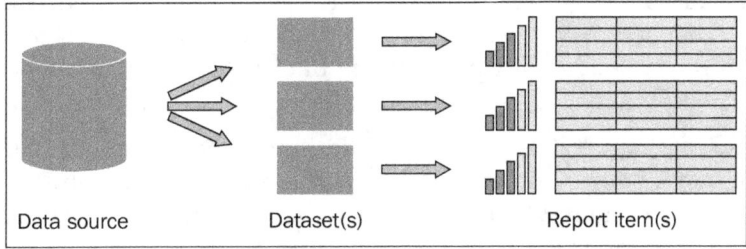

Relationship between primary report components

Report items can also be shared just like datasets and data sources. Shared report items, referred to as **report parts** can be based on either a shared dataset or an embedded dataset. When based on an embedded dataset, the dataset is wrapped up with the shared report part as a single unit and made available to other report developers. By creating shared report parts and reusing existing ones, the speed of report authoring can be greatly increased.

# SSRS – Standard Reporting

> Report items can be published to Report Server as report parts. Report authors using Report Builder to create new reports can save time by leveraging the existing report parts instead of recreating them in each report.
>
> The extended use and administration of shared report parts is a bit more complex than shared datasets and shared data sources, and outside the scope of this book. Please check out the following TechNet article for more information: http://technet.microsoft.com/en-us/library/ee633670.aspx

The following is a list of the report items available right out of the box with SSRS 2012 along with basic descriptions of each:

- **Textbox**: This is a basic freeform text object that can be placed anywhere on the report body as well as the header and footer areas. The text value displayed can be static or the result of an expression.
- **Line**: This is just a graphic for aesthetic purposes.
- **Table**: This is one of the primary report items most commonly used to display data from a dataset in the standard two-dimensional table format. Cells of the table typically contain text but can also contain a variety of other report items, such as data bars, sparklines, charts, and many others.
- **Matrix**: This report item is based on the same underlying structure as a table except that it comes with a row group and column group already defined. Use this component when you want to display data pivoted on columns as with crosstab reports.

> Table and matrix report items are based on the same underlying structure, which is known as the **tablix**. A table is a tablix without row/column groups, while a matrix is a tablix with row/column groups. See the following screenshot for an example of the differences while displaying data in a table (left) versus a matrix (right).

| Calendar Year | Month | Sales Amount | | Calendar Year | January | February | March | April | May |
|---|---|---|---|---|---|---|---|---|---|
| CY 2005 | July | $473,388 | | CY 2005 | | | | | |
| | August | $506,192 | | CY 2006 | $596,747 | $550,817 | $644,135 | $663,692 | |
| | September | $473,943 | | CY 2007 | $438,865 | $489,090 | $485,575 | $506,399 | |
| | October | $513,329 | | CY 2008 | $1,340,245 | $1,462,480 | $1,480,905 | $1,608,751 | |
| | November | $543,993 | | | | | | | |
| | December | $755,528 | | | | | | | |
| CY 2006 | January | $596,747 | | | | | | | |
| | February | $550,817 | | | | | | | |
| | March | $644,135 | | | | | | | |
| | April | $663,692 | | | | | | | |

Example of the differences when displaying data in a table (left) versus a matrix (right)

- **Rectangle**: This report item is a container used for grouping sets of report components placed within them. The group of report components can then be published to the report server as a single shared report part that can be reused in other reports. Rectangles can also be placed inside other report components such as the cells of a table.
- **List**: This report item, like the table and the matrix, is based on the underlying tablix data structure. The difference is that a list is used to create repeating areas in which additional report components can be placed in order to create what is known as a free-form report.
- **Image**: This report item is used to display a graphic, such as a company logo or product picture on the report. The image can be embedded in the report, but it is more common to have the image stored as a separate item on the report server, in a database, or somewhere out on the Web and then referenced from the report and displayed at runtime.
- **Subreport**: This report item is used to display the contents of another report (from the same report server) within the main report. The primary purpose of this report component is to promote encapsulation of information and reuse of existing development. However, from a performance perspective, it is typically a better idea to use the Nested Data Region design pattern, which you can read about in the following TechNet article: `http://technet.microsoft.com/en-us/library/dd207033.aspx`.

- **Chart**: This report item is used to provide a visual representation of the data in a report. The various types of charts available out of the box are shown in the following screenshot:

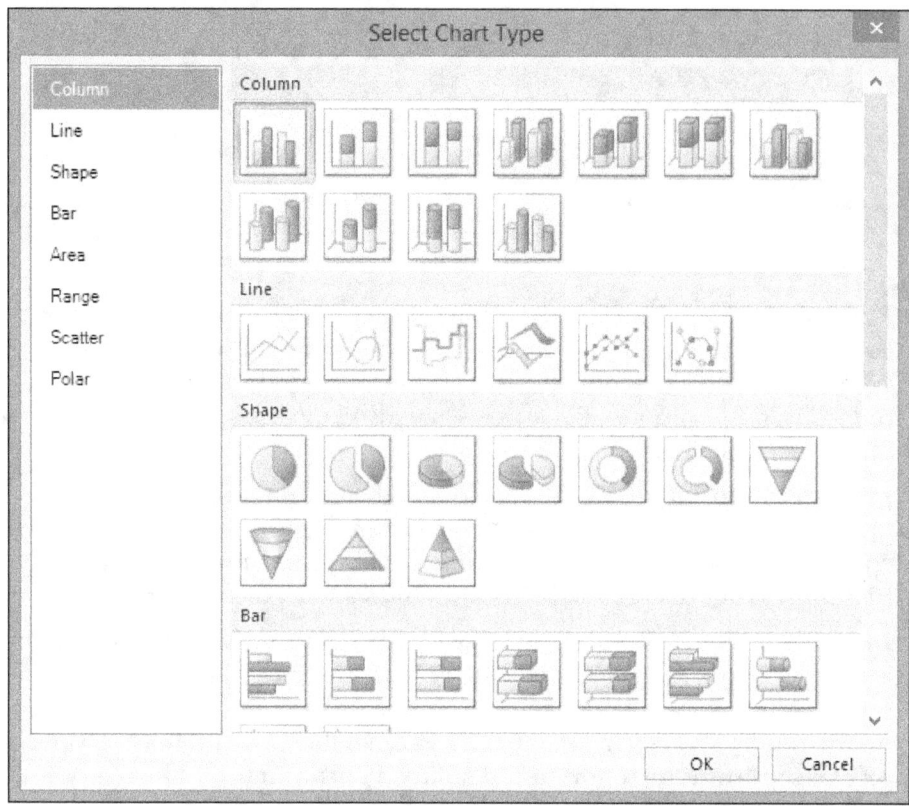

Options for chart report item

- **Gauge**: This report item is typically used to visualize **Key Performance Indicators (KPIs)** on a report. As you can see in the following screenshot, there are quite a few options available:

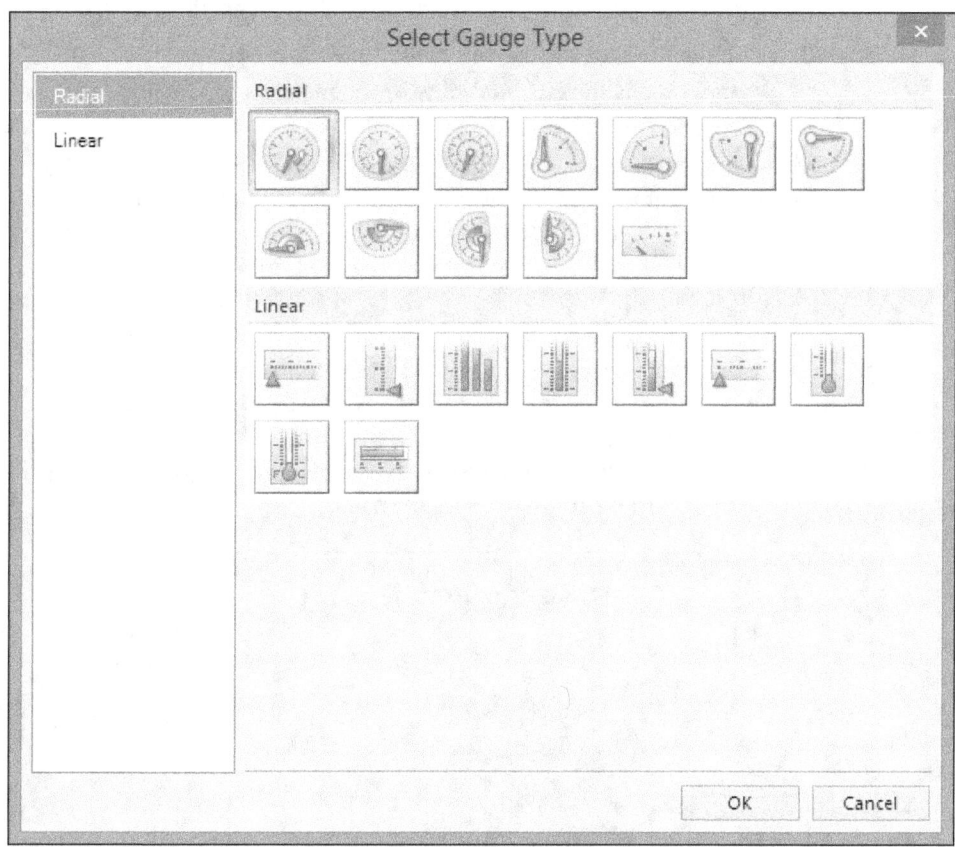

Options for gauge report item

>  A KPI is a type of metric consisting of three to four measures that together provide information on how well the business is progressing towards a goal. These are very common in Business Intelligence dashboards or summary reports.
>
> The following is a list of the measures that make up a KPI metric:
>
> - **Value**: This is the current value of the metric.
> - **Target**: This is the goal value.
> - **Status**: This is the value that provides context between the Value and Target measures. This is typically defined as a breakdown of ranges corresponding to bad (red), ok (yellow), and good (green).
> - **Trend**: This is the current trajectory based on recent history (optional).

- **Map**: This report item provides the ability to visualize information in a spatial or geographical context. There are typically two types of data involved with the map report item: spatial and analytical. Spatial data is required and provides the coordinates for layout. Analytical data is optional and provides the business measures or metrics.

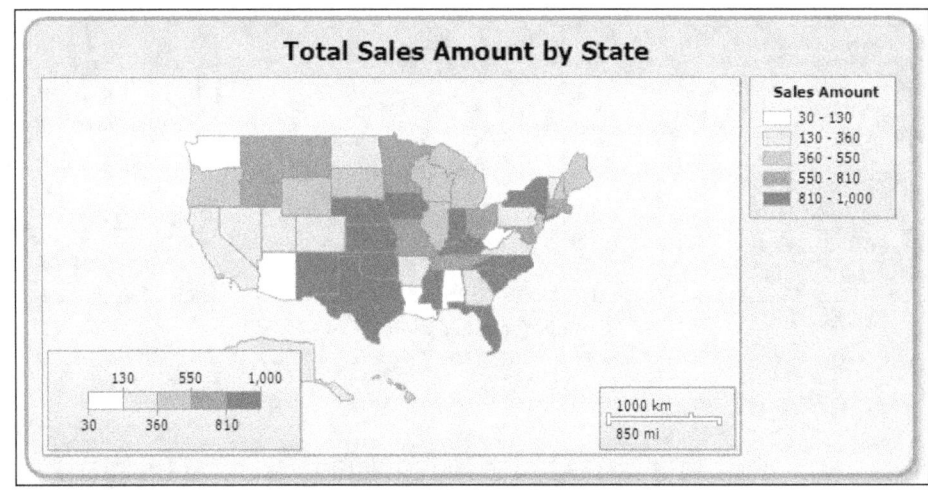

Example of map report item

- **Data bar**: This report item is typically used in conjunction with a table or matrix report item and is good for visualizing the relative strength/weakness of a metric or measure across a group of business entities such as sales territories.

- **Sparkline**: This report item is similar to the data bar in the way is used in conjunction with a table or matrix report item. However, the sparkline is more appropriate than the data bar to visualize trends or business measures over time.

| Country | YTD Total | | YTD Trend |
|---|---|---|---|
| Australia | | $3,033,784 | |
| United States | | $2,838,512 | |
| United Kingdom | | $1,298,249 | |
| Germany | | $1,058,406 | |
| France | | $1,026,325 | |
| Canada | | $535,784 | |

- **Indicator**: This is like the data bar and sparkline; this report item is commonly used in conjunction with a table or matrix and is used to visualize the status (and trend) of a business metric or KPI.

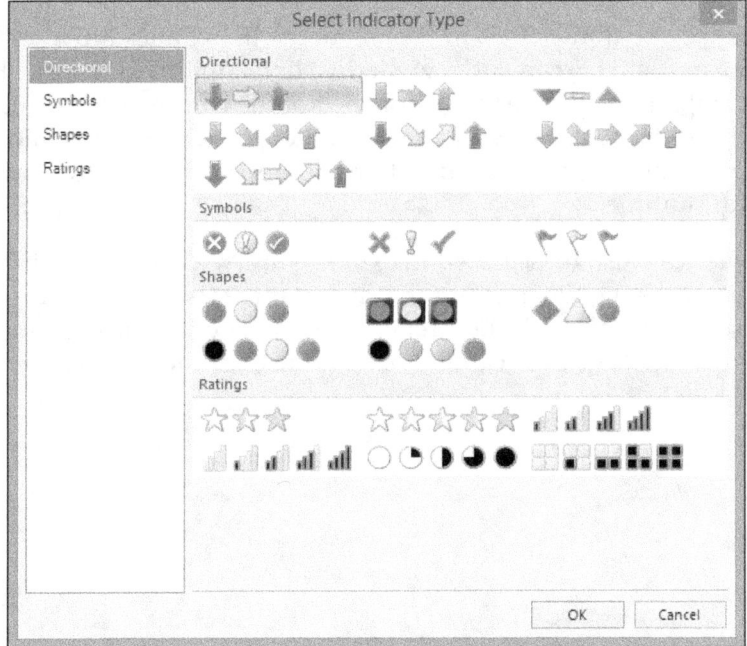

Options for indicator report items

In addition to the objects listed earlier, there are custom report items that you can obtain from third-party sources if the visualization required is not offered out of the box.

>  Choosing the correct report item depends heavily on the type of information you are trying to convey to the user. There is an entire field called DataViz, or Data Visualization, focused on optimizing this piece of the puzzle.

## Additional components of a report

A basic report can be created from just the primary components (data source, dataset, and report items) discussed in the previous section. However, in practice, there are a few other objects used to make reports more useful and flexible for business users.

## Report parameters

Parameters provide users with control over the behavior of a report at runtime. The most common use of parameters is in conjunction with a dataset to filter the results returned by the query. This can add a great deal of flexibility to reports. For example, instead of developing a separate report for each of the company's six sales territories, a single report could be created with a sales territory parameter that allows the user to choose the sales territory or subset of sales territories that they want data displayed for at runtime.

Parameter values can also be accessed in expressions (which will be discussed in the next section) allowing the user to provide input that is then used to set various properties at runtime. For example, a report parameter could be used to control the color scheme of a report or the visibility of a report item such as a chart.

The following is a screenshot of the general page when creating a report parameter:

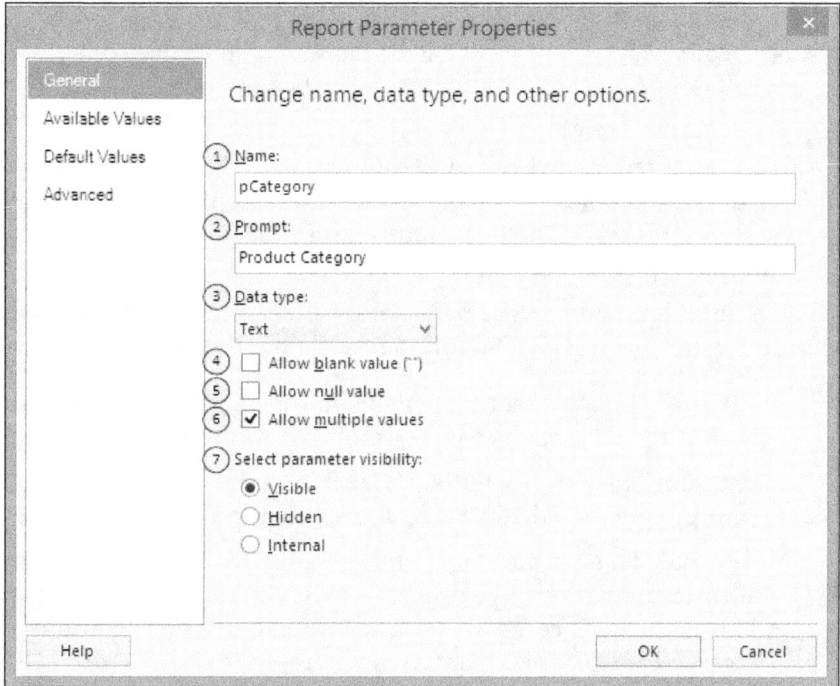

Report parameter properties dialog box

Let us have a look at these parameters:

- The area numbered **1** is **Name**. This is the name of the parameter that is used to reference the parameter from other objects in the report.
- The area numbered **2** is **Prompt**. This is the string that will be displayed to the user at runtime; it should be descriptive and intuitive.
- The area numbered **3** is **Data type**. This defines the type of data contained in the parameter value. Possible values include **Text**, **Boolean**, **Date/Time**, **Integer**, and **Float**.
- The area numbered **4** is **Allow blank value ("")**. This defines whether a parameter value can be left blank or not.
- The area numbered **5** is **Allow null value**. This defines whether a parameter value can be set to null.

>  The most common use for the **Allow blank value** and **Allow null value** options is when you want to make a parameter optional. Don't forget to handle the blank/null value scenarios if this parameter is referenced in the dataset query.

- The area numbered **6** is **Allow multiple values**. This property defines whether or not the parameter can contain multiple values. For example, enabling the user to run the report for a group of sales territories at the same time as opposed to a single sales territory.
- The area numbered **7** is **Select parameter visibility**. This section defines the visibility of the parameter. The following is a breakdown of the three options:
    - **Visible**: This parameter is visible to the user and can be manually set at runtime. This is the most common option for parameter visibility.
    - **Hidden**: This parameter is not visible to the user, but it can be set at runtime via the URL used to access the report on the report server.
    - **Internal**: This parameter is not visible to the user and cannot be set at runtime via the URL used to access the report on the report server. This is the least common parameter visibility option and is typically reserved for complex scenarios where, for example, the .NET report viewer control is embedded in a custom application to display reports to the user.

Parameters can be configured with a list of available values, which improves user experience. For example, when running a product detail report, instead of the user having to remember the exact name and spelling of the target product, a dataset can be created to retrieve a complete list of products from a relational database or SharePoint list. This dataset can then be tied to the report parameter and used to pre-populate the list of available values. The user can then select the target product from the list at runtime.

Parameters can also be configured with default values. If a default value is not supplied ahead of time, the report user must enter a value (or select a value from the list of available values) before the report can be executed. If default values have been defined for all parameters, then the report will begin executing immediately upon opening.

# Expressions

Expressions are snippets of custom logic that greatly enhance the report development process by providing a mechanism for developers to control nearly every aspect of a report. The pervasiveness of expressions throughout the report and all its underlying components is perhaps the number one factor in making SSRS the most customizable reporting technology in the Microsoft BI stack.

Expressions are written in Microsoft Visual Basic and can access context-specific constants, parameters, dataset values, common functions, and custom code in order to build the required logic. For example, the following screenshot shows an expression that controls the background color of the cells in a table based on the values of a field in the associated dataset:

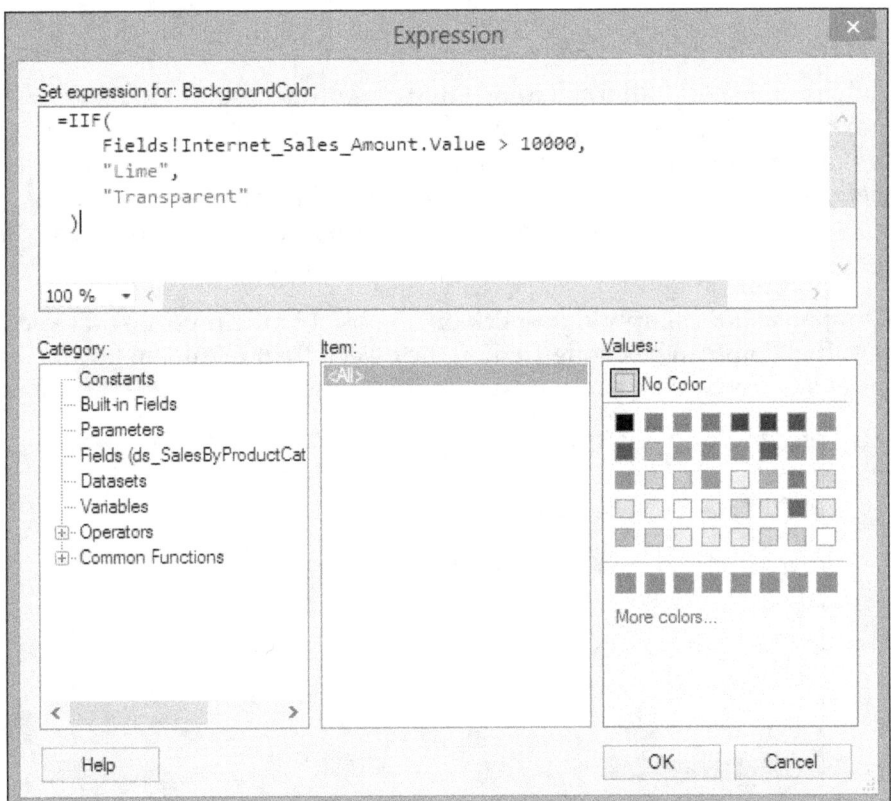

Example of an expression to control the background color of cell

The effects of the expression from the preceding screenshot can be seen in the following screenshot:

| Country | Sales Amount |
|---|---|
| Australia | $1,594 |
| Canada | $14,378 |
| France | $4,608 |
| Germany | $1,984 |
| United Kingdom | $4,279 |
| United States | $53,608 |

Result of the expression controlling the background fill color

# Actions

Actions are used to add additional interactivity and functionality to the user experience by allowing the report developer to define events that take place when users click on certain objects or areas displayed on a report. Actions can be defined on a variety of report items such as a textbox or cells in a matrix or table. They can also be defined on most charts and visual objects, such as data bars, gauges, and maps.

To configure an action, simply right-click on an object in the report, and select **Properties**. If actions can be configured on the object, then there will be an **Action** page such as the one shown in the following screenshot:

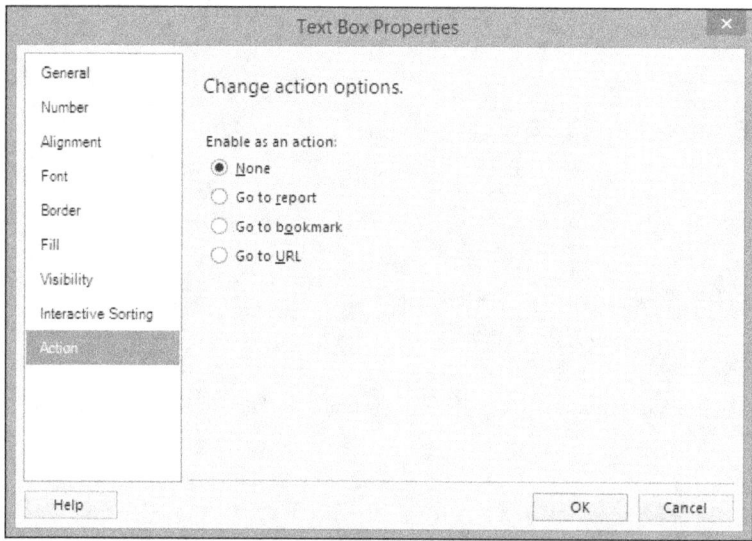

Action page of Text Box properties dialog box

There are three main types of actions that can be defined:

- **Go to report**: This action type allows the developer to define a separate report to display to the user when they click on the object that this action has been defined for. When creating this type of action, the developer must specify a report on the same report server and has the options of specifying parameter values to be passed to the target report. The **Go to report** action is most commonly used to build drill-through capabilities where a user starts out viewing a high-level summary report and then navigates to a detailed report by clicking on a specific object or field.

- **Go to bookmark**: This type of action allows the report user to navigate to a predefined bookmark within the same report when they click on the object that the action has been defined for. This action type is typically only used in longer reports made up of multiple logical sections and prevents users from having to scroll through many pages to get to the section of interest.

- **Go to URL**: This type of action allows the developer to define an URL that is displayed in the report user's default browser when they click on the object that the action has been defined for. For example, in a product detail report, a **Go to URL** action might be defined that when clicked, brings up the product specification page from the company's inventory website.

Parameters, Expressions, and Actions can be combined to create some really cool interactivity and a great user experience. For example, you might create a **Go to report** action on the bars of a bar chart and configure the target report to be determined based on the evaluation of an expression, which uses the value selected for a report parameter at runtime. This would allow the user to have control over the drill-through path when exploring complex hierarchies and relationships.

# Custom code

Custom code is a feature used to encapsulate complex logic so that it can be easily reused in expressions throughout a report or across multiple reports. Another popular use of custom code is to create a custom color scheme. Custom code comes in two flavors: embedded or external.

Embedded custom code is manually entered into the custom code box found on the **Code** page of the **Report Properties** window (which is shown in the next figure) and is ideal for scenarios where the logic is only needed in a few reports. The code must be written in Visual Basic but can access external libraries as long as they are added to the references page of the **Report Properties** window.

*SSRS – Standard Reporting*

On the other hand, if there are many reports that need access to this logic, it is better to go with External custom code. External custom code is created outside of the report—usually in a separate Visual Studio project—and deployed to the report server. The .NET assembly (*.dll file) is then linked on the references page of the **Report Properties** window. Now, when a change needs to be made to existing logic, it can be made in a single place instead of having to open and update every report. Another point worth mentioning is that external code can be written in any .NET language.

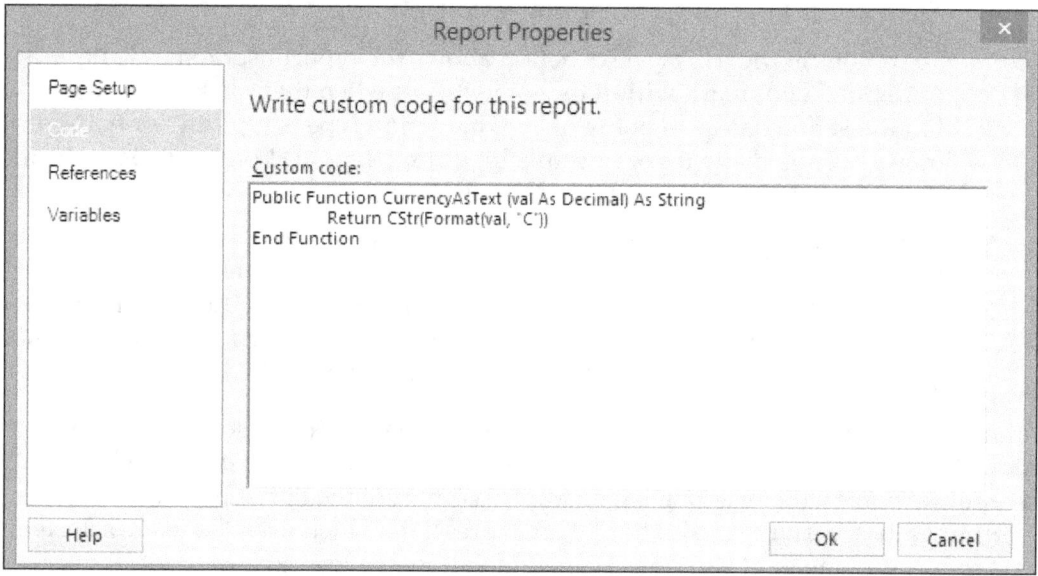

Example of embedded custom code

# Report development environment

There are two primary tools for report authors to use in creating SSRS reports: **Report Builder** and **Report Designer**.

- **Report Builder**: This is a standalone application offering a simplistic design experience and targeted at power users. This tool provides a familiar office-ribbon user interface and provides a wizard to guide the report author through the various report development tasks. It can also be used to easily edit existing reports that have been deployed to the report server.
- **Report Designer**: This is a fully featured report authoring tool based on Visual Studio and targeted at IT developers. Compared to Report Builder, this tool offers a much more manual development experience but can prove to be overly complicated for typical power users.

Feature-wise there is little difference between these two tools other than the ability to consume Shared Report Parts. Report Builder can be used to create and consume Shared Report Parts, while Report Designer can only be used to create and publish Shared Report Parts. However, from a development perspective, when you need to churn out a bunch of reports or when there are complex development scenarios (for example, subreports, drill-through requirements, and so on), it is usually easier to work in Report Designer.

## Server features and functionality

SQL Server Reporting Services is a server-based reporting system with an application layer responsible for the authentication, processing, rendering, and delivery of reports to users. Depending on the installation mode, the application layer might also be responsible for the security of reporting-related objects stored on the server such as reports, shared data sources, shared datasets, and shared report parts.

In addition to the items described below, which are fairly standard across most enterprise-level standard reporting systems, Reporting Services also includes a number of other features that provide substantial gains in performance and user experience. These features include items such as subscriptions, caching, and snapshots, as well as a new feature known as data driven alerts.

In the rest of this section, we will explore the primary server-level features and functionality offered by the SQL Server Reporting Services.

## Choosing an installation mode – SharePoint Integrated versus Native

While planning a SQL Server Reporting Services installation, you will need to choose between the Native and SharePoint Integrated modes. The report authoring and consumption experience is nearly identical between the two modes—and so the decision typically comes down to whether or not you already have an existing SharePoint farm or are planning to deploy one.

- **Native**: When this mode selected, a standalone web application is installed and provides a user interface to manage the configuration of the report server, folder and report settings, and security access controls. Users will typically access reports directly through the standalone report server.
- **SharePoint Integrated**: When this mode selected, the entire configuration, security access controls, and report rendering is managed through SharePoint. Users will typically access reports through SharePoint sites and document libraries.

From a feature perspective, there are only a few differences between Native and SharePoint Integrated mode. For example, Data Alerts are only available in SharePoint Integrated mode, while My Reports and Linked Reports are only available in Native mode. Each of these features will be discussed in more detail later in the chapter.

Both modes provide mechanisms for scaling out to accommodate a growing user load. See the following TechNet articles for details `http://technet.microsoft.com/en-us/library/hh479774.aspx` and `http://technet.microsoft.com/en-us/library/ms159114.aspx`.

## Scheduling

When it comes to standard reporting in general, the ability to schedule reports has become a ubiquitous feature in nearly all enterprise-level solutions; SQL Server Reporting Services is no exception. In the context of Reporting Services, a schedule is simply a request to automatically run a report at some point in the future. While a schedule is most commonly configured to execute on a regular, recurring basis, it can also be configured to execute a report just once and never again.

Reports can be associated with multiple schedules. For example, a report might be configured to run every weekday at 8 am (schedule 1) as well as every Sunday night at 10 pm (schedule 2).

Scheduling is available in both SharePoint Integrated and Native modes and comes in two forms: custom and shared. A custom schedule is a schedule created for a specific report and cannot be used by other reports on the report server. A shared schedule is a standalone, server-level object defined by a power user or administrator and can be used by multiple reports on the report server.

> One major requirement associated with scheduling is that the report must be configured to use either stored credentials or no credentials. Windows integrated security is not an option since the schedule is not associated with a user account, which can cause problems when trying to deal with dynamic data security.

The following screenshot shows the interface for creating a schedule on a report server installed in Native mode. The interface is similar in SharePoint Integrated mode:

**Schedule details**

Choose whether to run the report on an hourly, daily, weekly, monthly, or one time basis.
All times are expressed in (GMT -05:00) Eastern Standard Time.

○ Hour      **Daily Schedule**
◉ Day       ┌─────────────────────────────────────────────────────────┐
○ Week      │ ◉ On the following days:                                │
○ Month     │    ☐ Sun ☑ Mon ☐ Tue ☐ Wed ☐ Thu ☐ Fri ☐ Sat            │
○ Once      │ ○ Every weekday                                         │
            │ ○ Repeat after this number of days: [1]                 │
            │                                                         │
            │ Start time:  [08] : [00]       ◉ A.M.  ○ P.M.           │
            └─────────────────────────────────────────────────────────┘

**Start and end dates**

Specify the date to start and optionally end this schedule.

Begin running this schedule on: [11/20/2013                    ]
☐ Stop this schedule on:        [                              ]

[   OK   ]     [  Cancel  ]

There are three main uses for schedules in SSRS, which we will explore in the rest of this section:

- Subscriptions
- Snapshots
- Caching

One important distinction between these three items is that the first one is a business process enhancement, while the second and third items are performance enhancement techniques.

## Subscriptions

A subscription defines the execution and delivery of a report on a schedule. For example, a user might define a subscription to have a daily report executed each morning and delivered to their e-mail inbox so that they can review the information when they get into the office. This capability saves the business a lot of time because users are not required to manually navigate to the report server and run the reports every time they need to review the information to see how some aspect of the business is doing.

The following screenshot shows an example of a subscription to a daily sales report that runs every morning at 6 am and creates a PDF copy of the report on a network share; if the report contained parameters, values would need to be supplied at the time the subscription was created:

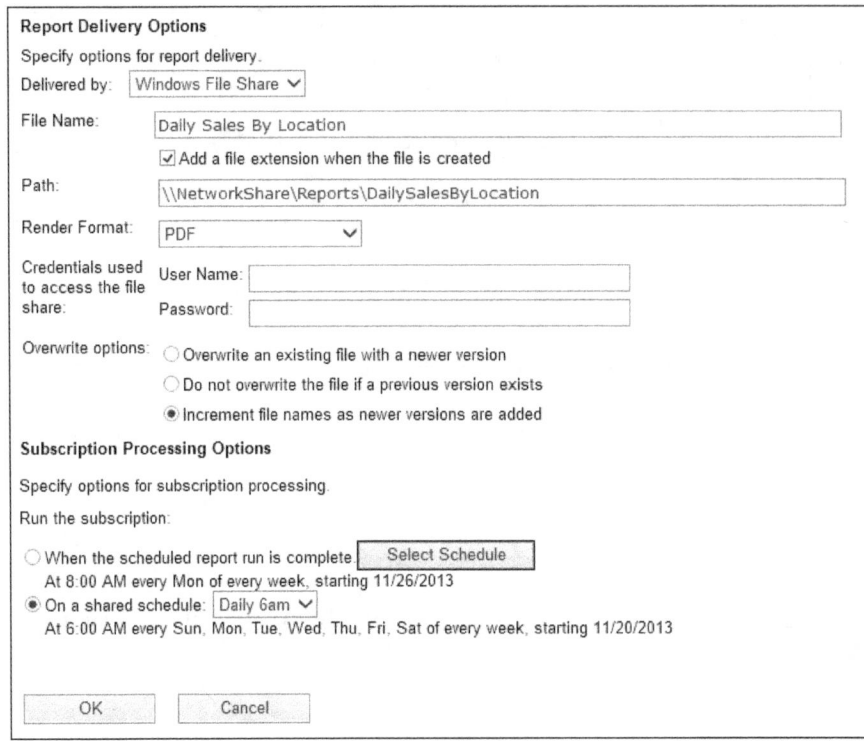

Report delivery options

There are four main report delivery options, and these define how the server should handle the results after executing the report.

- **Email**: Upon executing this option, the results are e-mailed to the recipient(s) in the form of a link to the report on the server or a physical file for offline viewing. A single subscription can be configured to e-mail multiple recipients.
- **Network File Share**: Upon executing this option, the report will be saved to the specified network file share for viewing in one of the available offline file formats.
- **SharePoint Document**: Upon executing this option, the report will be added to the specified SharePoint document library in one of the available offline file formats. This option is only available for report server installed in the SharePoint Integrated mode.

- **Null Delivery Provider**: This option is only used to preload the cache, which we'll cover later on in this chapter.

The following screenshot shows a list of the offline file formats available with Reporting Services 2012. For more information about these file formats, please see the following TechNet article at `http://technet.microsoft.com/en-us/library/ms154606.aspx`.

Subscriptions can be standard or data-driven. For standard subscriptions, all of the input parameters for the report (for example, **Sales Territory** and **Fiscal Period**) and the subscription (for example, recipient e-mail addresses and delivery file format) must be known and supplied at the time the subscription is created. With data-driven subscriptions, the values for parameters and delivery information are queried from a relational source when the schedule executes. This makes data-driven subscriptions ideally suited for delivering popular reports to a large list of recipients in a variety of formats with different runtime parameter values—especially if the list of recipients changes frequently.

>  While data-driven subscriptions offer a great deal of flexibility, they can be a bit complex to create and configure properly. Therefore, this task is usually taken on by a small handful of power users or members of the IT department.

## Report snapshots

The purpose of a snapshot is to reduce the load on the source system(s) and to reduce the time a report consumer waits for a long-running report to execute on demand. The basic idea is that a report is executed at some point in time, prior to when it is actually needed by the business. A copy of the execution results is stored as a snapshot on the report server. Then, at some point in the future, when users execute the same report, the request is satisfied from the existing snapshot instead of having to reprocess the entire report, which would involve sending another query to the source system(s) and processing the results again.

There is a tradeoff, however, for this performance gain. The data in a report generated from a snapshot will be stale; if the data in the source system(s) has changed since the snapshot was taken, the reports executed by the users that were satisfied by the snapshot will not contain the most recent changes. This is typically not a problem for summary reports or historical reports generated from a data warehouse. However, it could definitely be a problem if the purpose of the report is to provide up-to-the-minute information on a production line.

Enabling snapshots is done on a report-by-report basis. The first step is to change the **Processing Options** screen from the default setting of **Always run this report with the most recent data** to **Render this report from a report snapshot**. The next step is to actually create a snapshot, which can be done manually or on a schedule, though typically they are created and updated on a recurring schedule. The following screenshot is what the **Processing Options** screen should look like once both of these steps have been completed:

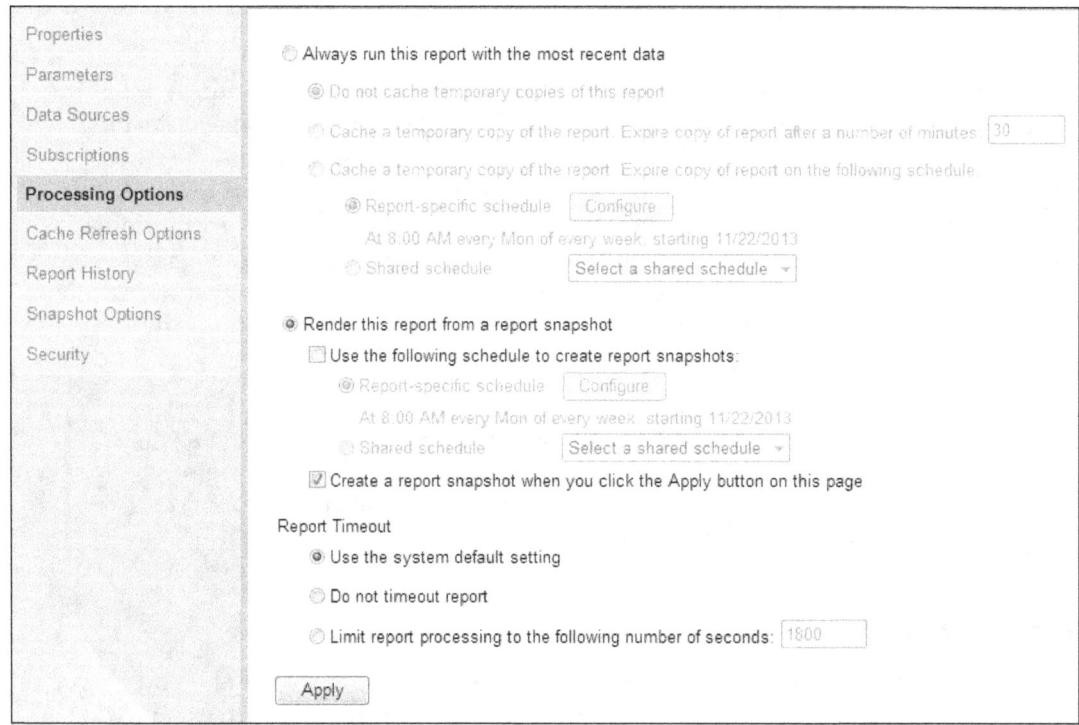

Report processing options

Before a snapshot can be created for a parameterized report, all parameters must be assigned default values. As long as users run the report using the default parameters, the request will be satisfied from the snapshot. However, if the users change the report parameters from the default values, utilization of the snapshot depends on how the parameter is used in the report. If the parameter is used in the dataset query to filter the results retrieved from the source system, the report will not be generated from the snapshot. However, if the parameter is used outside of the query to filter the dataset after all data has been retrieved from the source system, then the report will be generated from the snapshot. This makes sense because the snapshot is essentially storing the query results to avoid having to go back to the source system for different data, which is where the performance gains come from. Bottom line: as long as the query results don't change as a result of the parameter values, the snapshot will be utilized.

The following screenshot shows a simple table to help understand when a snapshot will be used:

|  | Default Parameter Values | Non-Default Parameter Values |
|---|---|---|
| Used In Query | Snapshot | No |
| Not Used In Query | Snapshot | Snapshot |

Snapshot usage table

A good use case for snapshots is period-end reports. These types of reports often deal with large amounts of data and can take a considerable amount of time to run. They are also characterized by their large audience of report consumers. Instead of having each user run this report on demand, a snapshot can be scheduled to run after hours as soon as the period ends. Then, when the users come in the next day, all subsequent requests can be satisfied immediately from the snapshot instead of having to wait for the data to be retrieved from the source system.

Snapshots are also a good way to maintain point-in-time views of the business. Building from the previous example of period-end reporting, the scheduled snapshots can be automatically saved in the report history providing a reference for how the business was performing at the end of each period.

Keep in mind that the default retention period for historical snapshots is 10 copies of the report. So if you have a monthly snapshot and need 12 months of historical snapshots, you will need to adjust this setting, which can be done at the server level (if you want it to apply to all reports) or at the individual report level.

 Once a report is configured to be rendered from a report snapshot, subscriptions can then be configured to execute every time an updated snapshot is created.

## Caching

The caching feature is very similar to snapshots in that it exists as a mechanism to improve report processing performance by keeping a stored copy of the report data and structure from which subsequent requests can be generated without having to go back to the source system. However, there are a few distinct differences you would do well to be aware of.

The main difference is that a cached copy of a report has a configurable lifespan. Once the cached copy of a report expires, the next execution of the report will run in its entirety — sending a query to the source system(s) to return up-to-date information to the user. This ability to control the lifespan of the cached copy of a report allows for a ceiling to be set for the maximum latency of the information contained in the report.

For example, the settings of a report can be configured such that the cached copy expires after 1 hour. During that 1-hour period after the cached copy is created, all executions of that report will be satisfied by the cached copy, and no query will be sent to the data source. After the 1-hour period has elapsed, the next user to execute the report will have to wait while the report is fully executed against the source system(s). That execution becomes the new cached copy from which all subsequent report requests are satisfied for the next hour.

The example scenario from the previous paragraph is not entirely accurate. It does not take into account parameterized reports and runtime parameter values, which is another difference between caching and snapshots. If you recall from the previous section, snapshots can only be created using the default parameter values. On the other hand, when caching is enabled, a separate cached copy of the report will be created for every combination of parameter values with which the report is executed. This may or may not be a desirable behavior. For example, if a report is structured such that there are many combinations of parameter values and each combination is typically only executed a few times, then the cached copies will rarely be used to satisfy a report execution request, which means most report executions will issue a query against the source system and users will be forced to wait for a full execution of the report. Furthermore, there is the additional overhead of storing the cached copies of each version of the report with very little benefit.

The two most common methods to expire cached copies of a report are through a recurring schedule or a configurable duration. The third option is to configure a cache refresh plan (shown in the following screenshot), which runs on a recurring schedule and updates the cached copy. The drawback with using cache refresh plans to keep the cached copies updated is that you must create one for every combination of parameters which could add considerable setup and maintenance overhead.

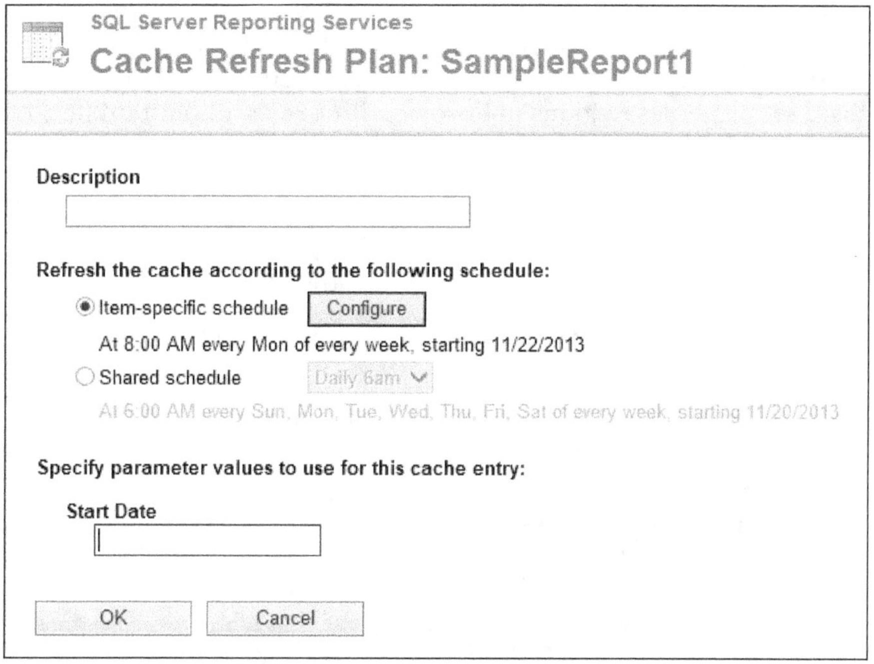

Example of cache refresh plan

You can learn more about caching reports from the TechNet article at http://technet.microsoft.com/en-us/library/ms155927.aspx.

# Data alerts

Data alerts are a brand new feature in SQL Server Reporting Services 2012 that allows business users to define custom alerts when information contained in a report changes or crosses a configured threshold. As mentioned in the section *Choosing an installation mode – SharePoint Integrated versus Native* earlier, this feature is only available for installations in the SharePoint Integrated mode.

Data alerts remove the need for business users to review a stack of standard reports each day, searching for specific events or conditions that require action or intervention on their part. Instead, business users can simply set up a few data-driven alerts based on customizable rules that match the events or conditions that they are responsible for. When the alert is triggered, an e-mail will be sent to the user with a description of the issue and a link to the report that the alert was generated from. The user can then review the data and take the necessary actions.

The following screenshot shows an example of a data alert being defined for the **Sales Amount By Sales Territory** report. The alert is configured to check every day to see if there are any Sales Regions in Europe with a sales amount under $1,000,000.

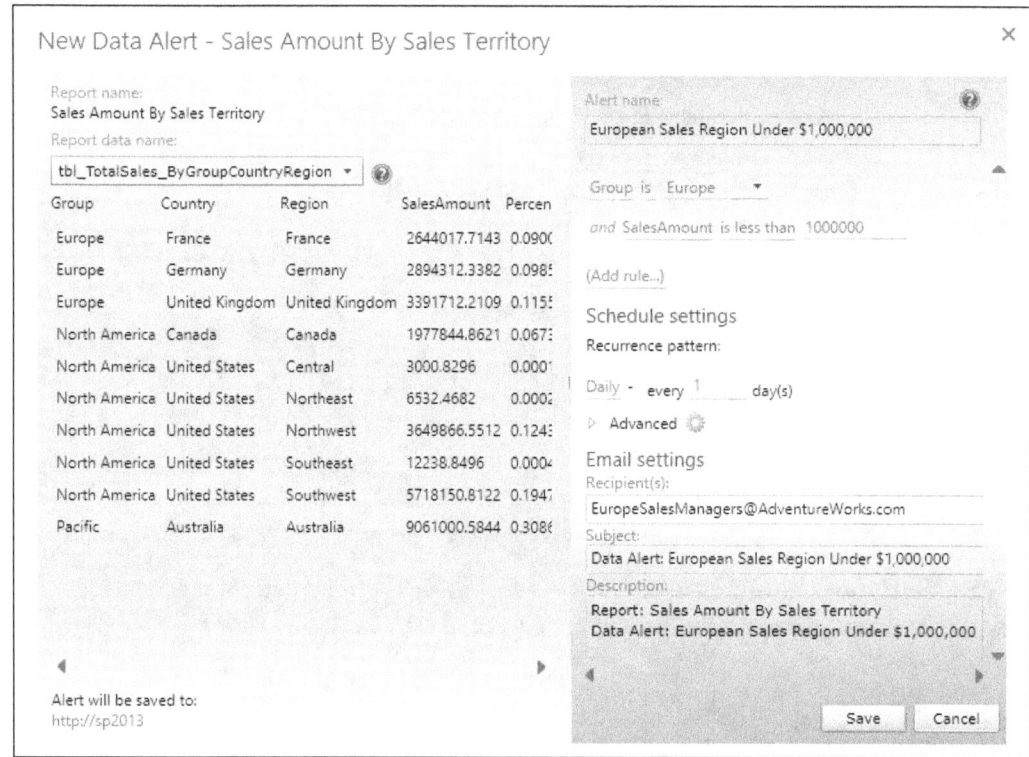

Example of a data alert

The primary components of a data alert are as follows:

- **Report data name**: This is the report item (table, chart, and so on) on which the alert will be based. Users select the report item from a pre-populated drop-down list.
- **Alert name**: This is the name of the alert and should describe the event being monitored.

- **Rule**: This defines the criteria that an alert will be triggered for. The UI provides the ability to define simple or complex rules based on any of the fields available in the underlying dataset for the selected report item. It also takes into account the data types of the fields contained in the dataset in order to provide intuitive options to define the rules. For example, when defining a rule involving a numeric field, the user will see a different set of comparison operators (for example, greater than, less than) than when the rule involves a text/string field.
- **Schedule settings**: This section is where the user configures the frequency at which to evaluate the rule criteria. Start and end dates can also be defined to constrain alert to run only during a relevant time period.
- **Email settings**: This section is where users define the recipient list and details to include in the notification e-mail. Along with the subject and description of the alert, a link to the report that the alert was generated from will all be included in the e-mail message.

> Using good naming conventions for report item and data fields during development will make it easier for business users to define data alerts.

The **Data Alert Manager** page shown in the following screenshot can be used to manage existing data alerts. Regular users will only have access to the alerts they create, while site administrators will have access to all alerts created by all users.

Data Alert Manager

Data alerts work by running stripped-down copies of the reports on the recurring interval defined in the alert schedule and evaluating the data returned against the rule criteria. Across an entire user base, the additional load of alerts can be considerable. Therefore, business users should be trained to set appropriate schedules for the data-driven alerts they create. For example, an alert for a weekly sales report does not need to be set to run every minute. In addition to training users on appropriate alert usage, administrators should be reviewing data alerts on a regular basis to ensure the frequencies are appropriately configured.

# My Reports (Native mode only)

My Reports is a feature that provides business users with a place on the report server where they can store and manage personalized reports. It is a server-wide setting that is disabled by default. The feature can be enabled by logging in to the Reporting Services instance through **SQL Server Management Studio (SSMS)** and using the server properties shown in the following screenshot:

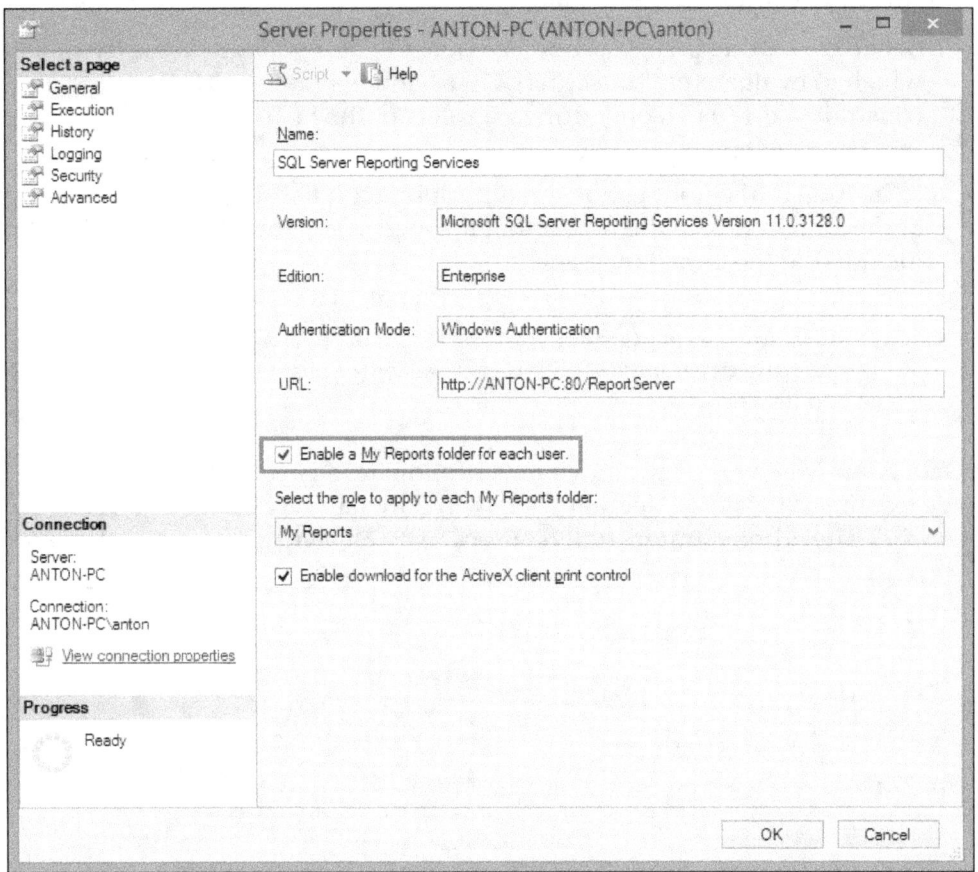

SSRS Server properties via SQL Server Management Studio (SSMS)

Once enabled, each user accessing the report server will have a folder named **My Reports** on the main page of the report server as shown in the preceding screenshot, in which they can create and store reports.

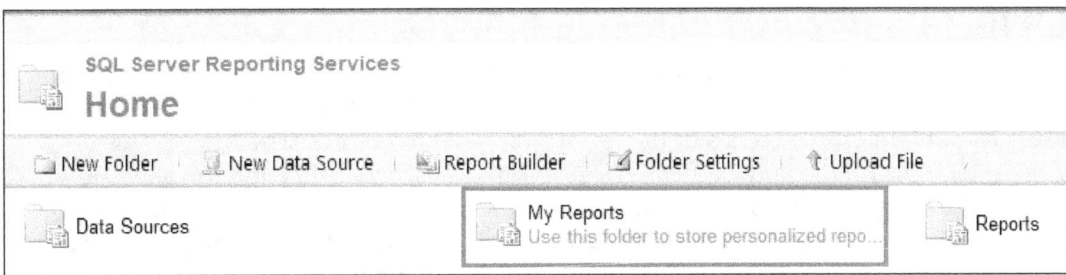

My Reports folder after enabling feature at server level

Regular users only have access to their own **My Reports** folder, while report server administrators will be able to view all folders.

## Linked reports (Native mode only)

A linked report is basically just a shortcut to another report on the report server. Users with appropriate permissions can create linked reports and save them to another folder, such as My Reports, on the report server.

One very useful characteristic of linked reports is that they can have their own configurations—completely separate from the original copy. This means that linked reports can have different default parameters, run on different schedules, have different snapshot or cache configurations, and so on.

## Consuming reports

There are a number of ways for users to consume Reporting Services reports.

## Online

For on-demand scenarios the most common method is to view the reports online using a browser through the reporting services web application, SharePoint site, or through a custom application that interfaces with the report server. Another scenario where users will typically view a report online is with data alerts. When a data alert is triggered, the generated e-mail sent to the user will contain a link to the source report.

# Offline

There are plenty of scenarios where users might need to view standard reports in an offline format through applications such as Microsoft Excel or Word. In these cases, users can obtain offline copies of the report in one of two ways. The first way is to view the report online and export a copy of it in one of the offline file formats shown in the following screenshot. The other method to view a report offline is to set up a subscription to execute the report and deliver it to a specified destination such as a network file share, e-mail inbox, or SharePoint document library.

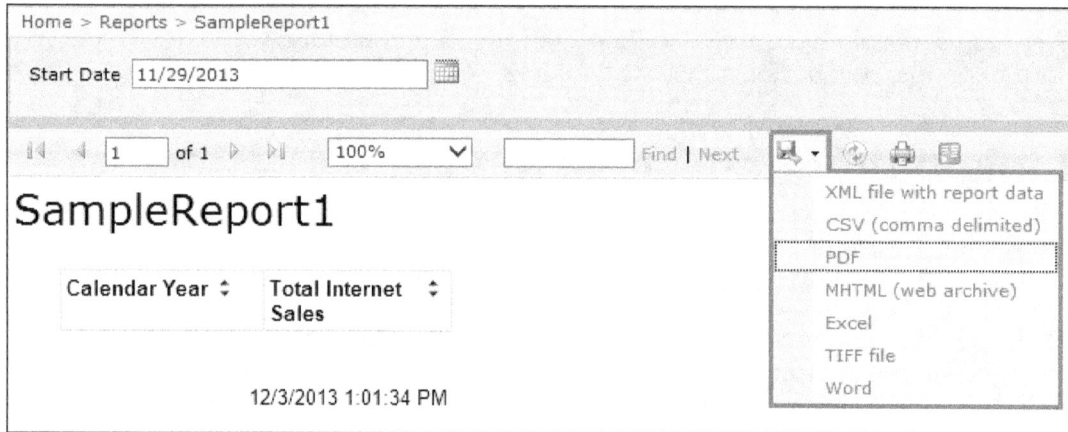

Export options from within report viewer

# Data feed

Reporting Services reports can also be consumed as a data feed by other applications that support Atom-compliant data feeds. You can learn more about generating data feeds from reports in the TechNet article at http://technet.microsoft.com/en-us/library/ee240754.aspx.

# Extensibility

SQL Server Reporting Services is a very extensible product that provides a number of interfaces through which custom applications can leverage or expand upon existing features and functionalities. For more detailed information, please refer to the TechNet article at http://technet.microsoft.com/en-us/library/bb522713.aspx.

# Security

Security is a very important part of an enterprise-level standard reporting infrastructure. Reporting Services provides a variety of options and capabilities for securing objects on the report server as well as the information displayed in the reports.

> This section discusses security at a high level. For a deeper understanding and a complete list of differences between Reporting Services in the Native and SharePoint Integrated modes from a security perspective, please refer to the section on TechNet at `http://technet.microsoft.com/en-us/library/bb522824.aspx`.

## Roles and permissions

Access to objects on a report server, such as reports, shared data sources, shared datasets as well as features and functionality such as creating a subscription or a data alert, is controlled through roles. Roles are predefined sets of permissions that can be granted to users or user groups.

Reporting Services comes with a set of standard roles, each of which is defined to target a specific type of user. For example, the **Browser** role is typically assigned to any user who simply needs to be able to run reports, while the **Content Manager** role is reserved for power users or report administrators.

You can learn more about the default roles from the following TechNet articles:

- SharePoint Integrated Mode
  (`http://technet.microsoft.com/en-us/library/bb326284.aspx`)
- Native Mode
  (`http://technet.microsoft.com/en-us/library/ms157363.aspx`)

> In SharePoint Integrated mode, roles are referred to as permission levels, but conceptually they are the same. The following TechNet article contains a comparison of the standard roles between the two different installation modes: `http://technet.microsoft.com/en-us/library/bb283182.aspx`.

Report server administrators can customize existing roles or create new roles if the default roles do not meet the requirements of your environment. For example, in a SharePoint Integrated mode environment, you may have users who need to be able to view reports and create subscriptions and alerts, but you don't want them to be able to create new reports. This would require a custom role or permission level because the viewer/read permission level does not allow users to create subscriptions or data alerts and the next level up; members/contribute permission level allows users to create reports.

## Securing Report Server objects

Objects that reside on the report server, such as shared data sources, shared report parts, and reports, are all secured like files on a Windows filesystem. Permissions to access an object can be granted directly on the object, or it can be granted at the folder level giving users access to all objects contained within the folder. These permissions are, of course, granted to the user on the object or folder through roles as we learned in the previous section.

By default, role assignments and permissions are inherited from the top-level down. Say, for example, the **Report Server** folder structure resembles the diagram in the following figure, where a folder named **Reports** is the top level and contains three subfolders (**Finance**, **Sales**, and **Production**). If a user or group is given access to the **Reports** folder at the top level, they will by default have access to reports contained in all three subfolders. If, however, the user or group is only given access to the **Sales** folder, they will only have access to objects in that folder and any subfolders beneath—they will not have access to reports contained in any of the other folders at the same level or above.

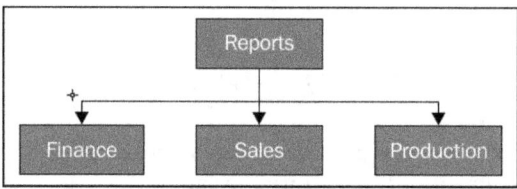

Changing the permissions at lower levels will break the chain of inheritance. The following scenario will help to illustrate this effect:

1. Bob is granted the Publisher role on the top-level **Reports** folder.
2. Bob's permissions on the **Finance** folder are changed to Browser.
3. Bob is granted the Report Builder and Content Manager roles on the top-level **Reports** folder.

After item 1, Bob has Publisher rights on the top-level **Reports** folder and (because of inheritance) he also has publisher rights on the **Finance**, **Sales**, and **Production** subfolders.

After item 2, Bob still has publisher rights on the top-level **Reports** folder and the **Sales** and **Production** subfolders. But now he only has Browser rights on the **Finance** folder.

After item 3, Bob has Publisher, Report Builder, and Content Manager rights on the top-level **Reports** folder, as well as the **Sales** and **Production** subfolders. On the **Finance** folder, he still only has browser rights.

If a report references external objects such as a shared data source or shared dataset, then users will need permissions to those items as well—even if they are located in a separate folder.

## Data security

In addition to controlling server-level capabilities (for example, creating subscriptions and data alerts) and Report Server objects (for example, reports, shared data sources, and shared datasets), Reporting Services also provides several mechanisms for controlling the data displayed in reports—also known as row-level security. A typical scenario would be to limit the data in the daily sales report so that each sales manager can only see data for their territory. Instead of creating multiple reports (one for each sales territory) and managing access to each on the report server (so that each sales manager only has access to the report for his or her territory), we can create a single daily sales report and use dynamic row-level security.

One way to accomplish this is to use the **Windows Authentication** option for the credentials of the report data source(s). This works by using the credentials of the user running the report to authenticate with the source system. The source system can then extract the username from the connection and use it to filter the results of a query so that only the appropriate data is returned from the source system to the report.

 How the username is extracted from the connection to the source system depends on the source system. For example, if the source system is a SQL Server database, then the USER_NAME() function will return a string in the form of DOMAIN\USERNAME. On the other hand, if the source system is an Analysis Services cube, then the USERNAME() function can be used.

The significant consideration with this method is that certain reporting features (for example, subscriptions) require the data sources to use stored credentials. In this case, the credentials used to connect to the source system will be those of the account stored with the data source—typically a common service credential. The `User!UserId` function can then be used to obtain the `DOMAIN\USERNAME` of the user running the report and passed as a parameter in the query against the source system to filter the data according to the user running the report.

# Summary

In this chapter, we covered the main features and functionalities offered in SQL Server Reporting Services 2012, including a breakdown of report components, development experience, extensibility, and security. By now, readers should have a general understanding of the capabilities offered in SQL Server Reporting Services. In the next chapter, we are going to roll up our sleeves and step into the shoes of a report developer to create a report and deploy it to a report server.

# 3
# Development Activity with SSRS

In this chapter, we'll walk through the process of creating a basic **SQL Server Reporting Services** (**SSRS**) report. As we learned in the previous chapter, there are two tools we can use to create SSRS reports: Report Builder and Report Designer. We will be using Report Designer in **SQL Server Data Tools** (**SSDT**), which comes with the SQL Server 2012 installation media. After the report is created, we will deploy it to a local report server installed in Native mode.

The development activity in this chapter is broken up into the following sections:

- Creating a Reporting Services project
- Creating a report object
- Creating a shared data source
- Adding reference to the shared data source
- Creating a dataset
- Adding a report item
- Deploying a report project

## Prerequisites

Before you start this exercise, you will require the following prerequisites:

- Access to a Microsoft SQL Server 2012 Reporting Services report server installed in the Native mode with the appropriate permissions required to deploy reports and shared data sources

- Access to a Microsoft SQL Server 2012 Database Engine instance with the Adventure Works DW 2012 sample database deployed
- SQL Server Data Tools (SSDT) or Visual Studio 2010

Microsoft SQL Server 2012 is available in a 180-day trial version (which includes SQL Server Data Tools) from the location at http://www.microsoft.com/en-us/download/details.aspx?id=29066 and Adventure Works DW 2012 sample database is available for download from the location at http://msftdbprodsamples.codeplex.com/releases/view/55330.

## Tutorial scenario

In this exercise, you will step into the shoes of an IT developer working at a fictitious bike retailer called Adventure Works. You have been tasked with creating a report for the Internet sales department that will provide information on year-over-year sales trends. After developing the report, you will need to deploy it to the company's existing standalone report server, where it can be accessed by users in the sales department.

## Creating a Reporting Services project

Since we are using SQL Server Data Tools (instead of Report Builder) for this exercise, the first step is to create a Reporting Services project:

1. Open SQL Server Data Tools (SSDT).
2. From the menu bar across the top, navigate to **File** | **New** | **Project**.
3. In the **New Project** window, navigate to **Business Intelligence** | **Reporting Services** | **Report Server Project**.
4. Enter a name and location for the project, and click on **OK** to create and open the project.

*Chapter 3*

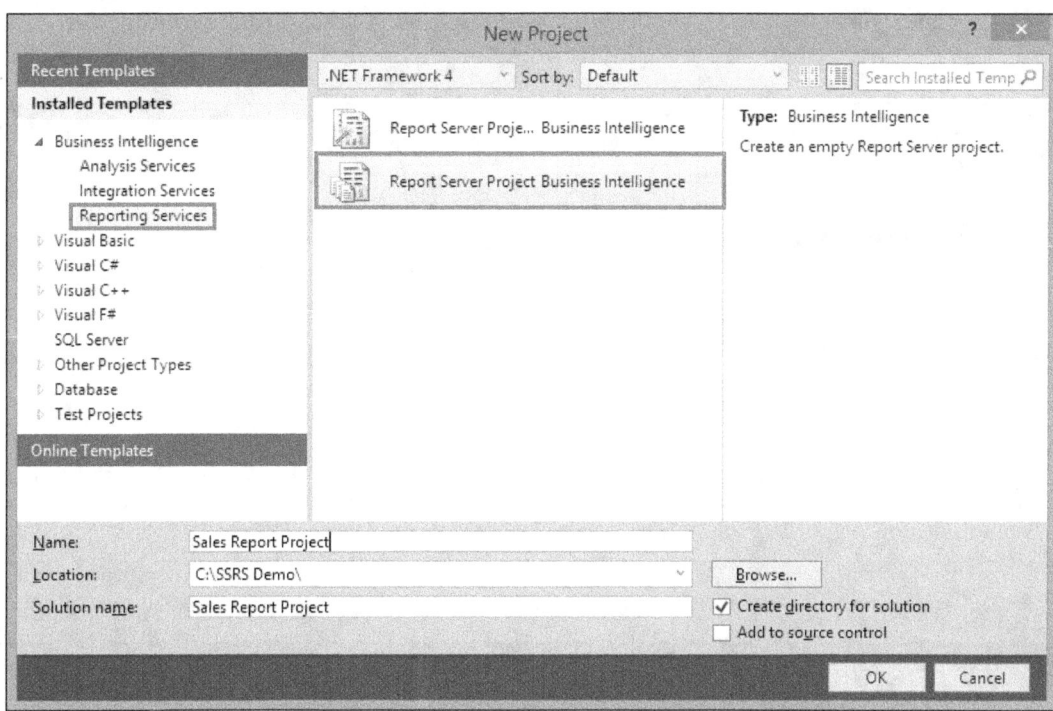

New Project dialog box for creating a new Report Server Project

## Creating a report object

After creating the project, you are ready to begin building your Reporting Services report as follows:

1. If necessary, open the **Report Server Project** created in the previous section.
2. In the **Solution Explorer** window, right-click on the `Shared Data Sources` folder, choose **Add**, and then select **New Item...** to bring up the **Add New Item** window as shown in the following screenshot.
3. Select **Report**.

4. Name the report `Sales Summary`, and click on **Add** to finish creating the report item, then add it to the **Report Server Project**.

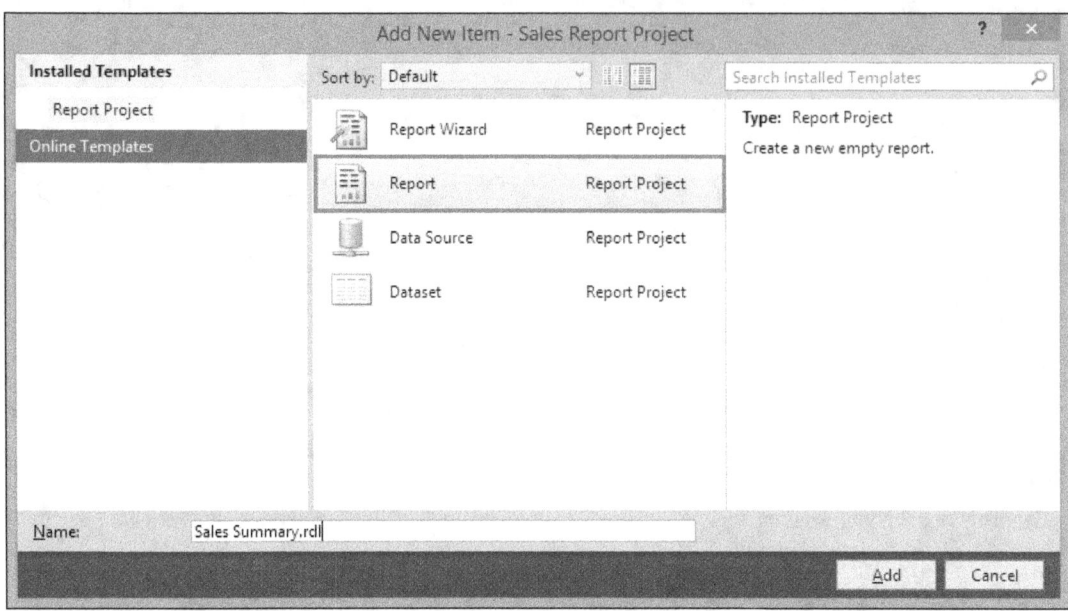

Add New Item dialog box for adding a new report to the Report Server Project

## Creating a shared data source

Next, you need to create a data source that contains the connection details to the source system that contains the Internet sales data on which you need to report. As you learned in *Chapter 2, SSRS – Standard Reporting*, there are two types of data sources: shared data sources and embedded data sources. For this exercise, you will create a shared data source pointing to the Adventure Works Sample Data Warehouse database, as follows:

1. In the **Solution Explorer** window, right-click on the `Shared Data Sources` folder, and choose **Add New Data Source**.
2. Name the data source `DW_AdventureWorks`, and confirm that Microsoft SQL Server is selected as the type of data source.
3. Click on the **Edit** button to bring up the **Connection Properties** dialog box shown in the following screenshot.
4. For the **Server name** property, enter the name of the server or SQL Server instance that hosts the source database.

5. In the **Connect to a database** section, select the source database from the drop-down list.
6. Click on the **Test Connection** button to make sure everything has been entered correctly.
7. Click on **OK** to save the changes and return to the **Shared Data Source Properties** window.
8. Select the **Credentials** page on the left to review the credentials used for this data source. Make sure **Use Windows Authentication** is selected and click on **OK** to create the shared data source. Using Windows authentication will ensure that only those users who have been granted access to the source database will have access to the data through this data source:

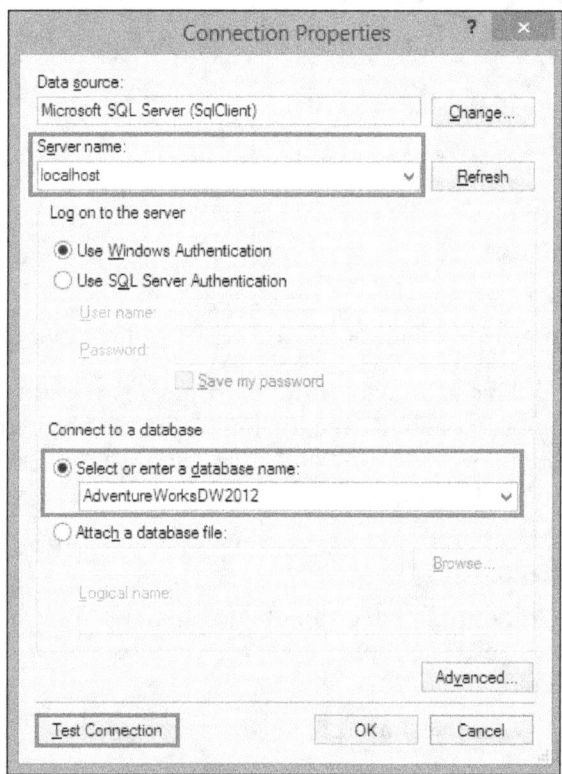

Connection Properties dialog box

# Adding reference to shared data source

At this point, the **Sales Summary** report and the `DW_AdventureWorks` shared data source are still two completely separate objects. In order to actually use the shared data source in the report, you need to create a data source reference in the report and point it to the shared data source in our project.

1. Open the **Sales Summary** report.
2. In the **Report Data** window, shown in the following screenshot, right-click on the `Data Sources` folder and select **Add Data Source...**.

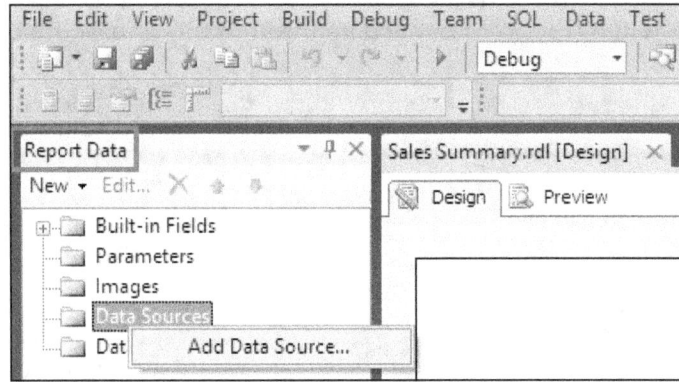

Report Data window in SQL Server Development Tools environment

3. In the **General** tab of the **Data Source Properties** window, as shown in the following screenshot, give the data source a name (for example, `sds_DW_AdventureWorks`), and select **Use shared data source reference**, as shown in the following screenshot.
4. Next, choose the shared data source created in the previous task from the drop-down menu.
5. Click on the **Credentials** tab and notice that all options are grayed out. This is because the credentials for shared data sources are controlled at the project level.
6. Click on **OK** to add the shared data source reference to the report.

*Chapter 3*

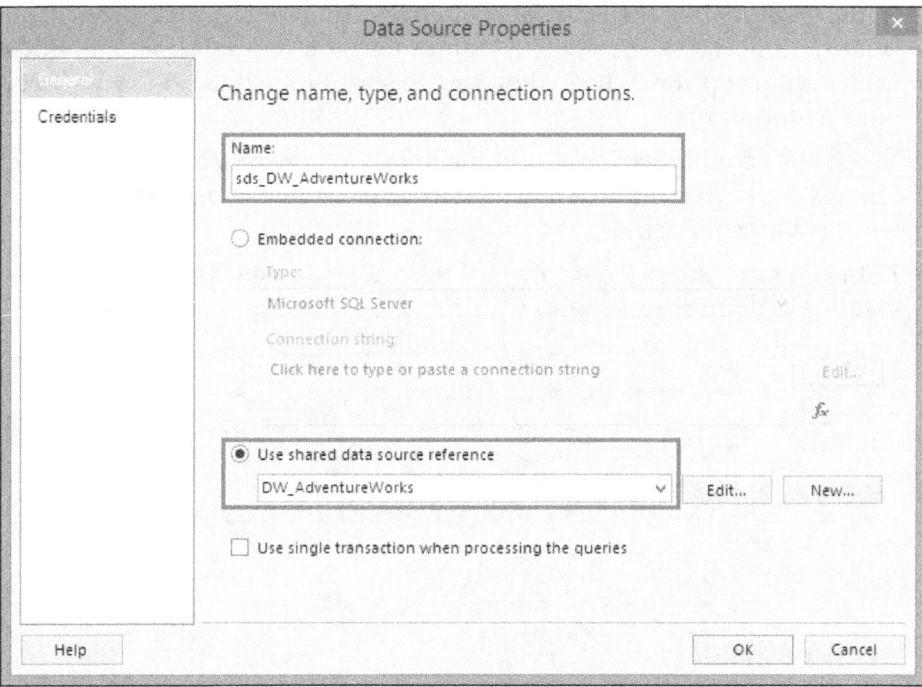

Data Source Properties dialog box

## Creating a dataset

The next step is to create a dataset. As you can recall from the previous chapter, the dataset is the component that holds the data pulled from source system. Follow these steps to create an embedded dataset to hold the **Sales Summary** data:

1. In the **Report Data** window, right-click on the Datasets folder, and select **Add Dataset…**.

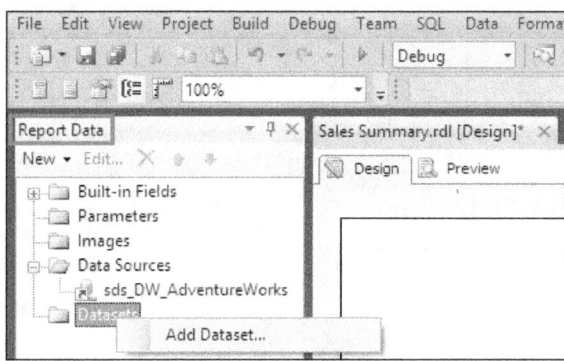

Report Data window in SQL Server Development Tools environment

## Development Activity with SSRS

2. In the **Query** tab of the **Dataset Properties** window, give the dataset a name (for example, `ds_SalesSummary`), and select the **Use a dataset embedded in my report option**, which allows us to specify the dataset via a query or stored procedure.

3. In the **Data source** section, select the data source reference (for example, `sds_DW_AdventureWorks`) from the drop-down list of available data sources in the report.

4. In the **Query** textbox, enter the following text, and click on **OK** to finish creating the embedded dataset:

```
SELECT    dd_ord.CalendarYear
         ,dd_ord.MonthNumberOfYear
         ,dd_ord.EnglishMonthName AS [Month]
         ,SUM(fis.SalesAmount) AS [TotalSalesAmount]
FROM     dbo.FactInternetSales fis
         INNER JOIN dbo.DimDate dd_ord ON dd_ord.DateKey = fis.OrderDateKey
GROUP BY dd_ord.CalendarYear
        ,dd_ord.MonthNumberOfYear
        ,dd_ord.EnglishMonthName
```

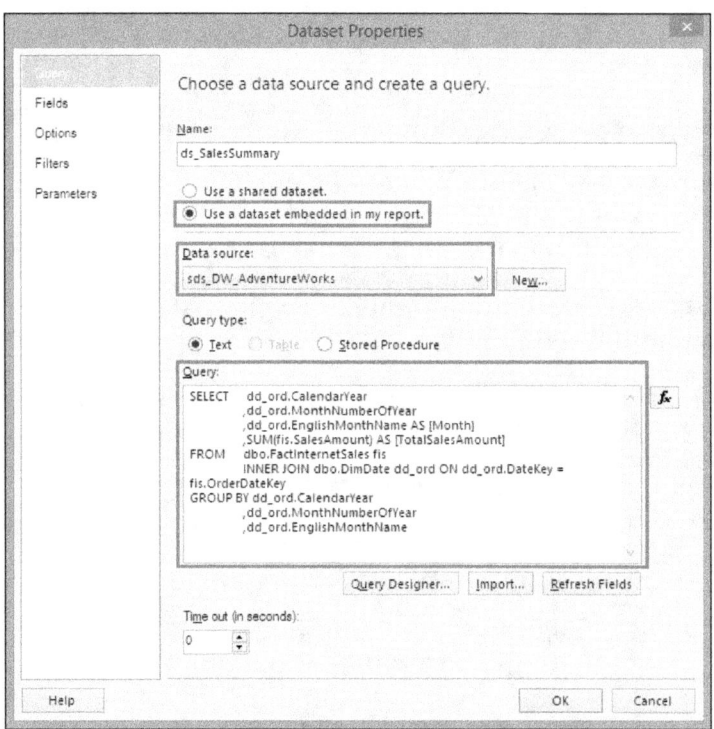

Dataset Properties dialog box

[ 60 ]

# Adding a report item

Now that the report contains a data source and a dataset, you are ready to create a report item to display the data in a meaningful way on the report. In this exercise, you will create a line chart to display year-over-year sales trends.

1. Right-click in a blank area of the report body, and navigate to **Insert | Chart**.
2. Select the first option in the **Line** section, and click on **OK** to create a **Line Chart** report item, as shown in the following screenshot:

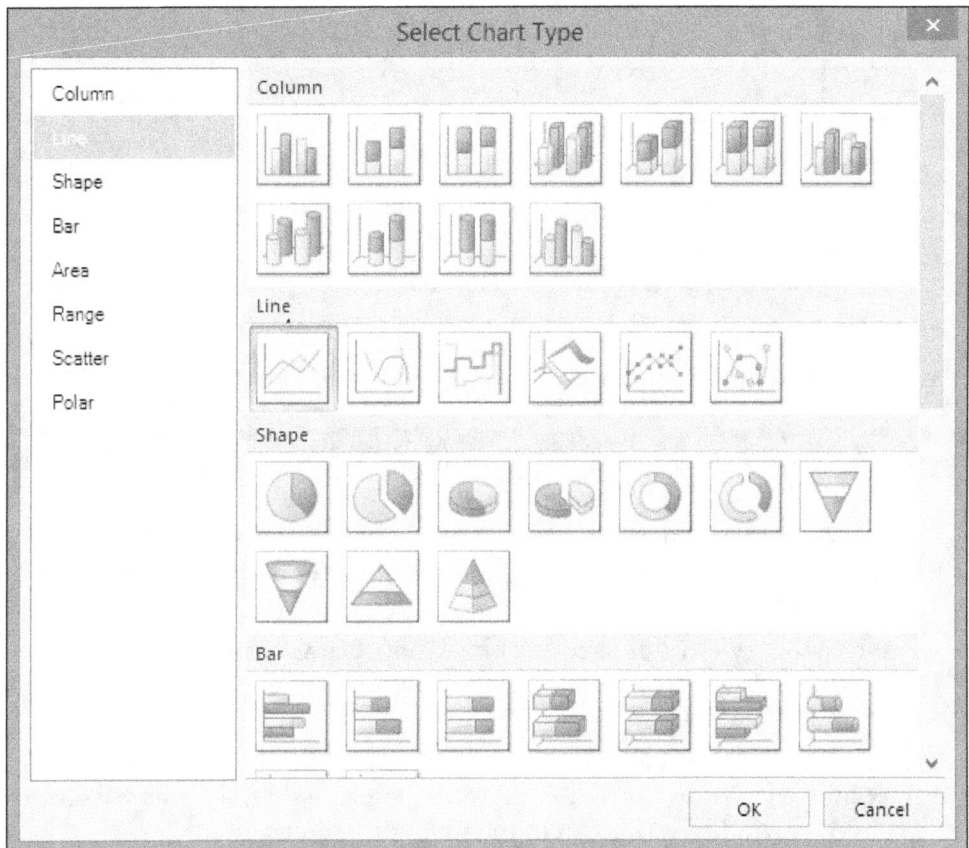

3. Click on the chart item that was created on the report body, move it to the upper-left corner of the report canvas, and then drag out the bottom-right corner to make the chart larger.

*Development Activity with SSRS*

4. Now, double-click on the chart item that was created on the report canvas; notice the **Chart Data** configuration box that appears to the right. Most report items, such as data bars, spark lines, and gauges, have configuration boxes like the one shown in the following screenshot:

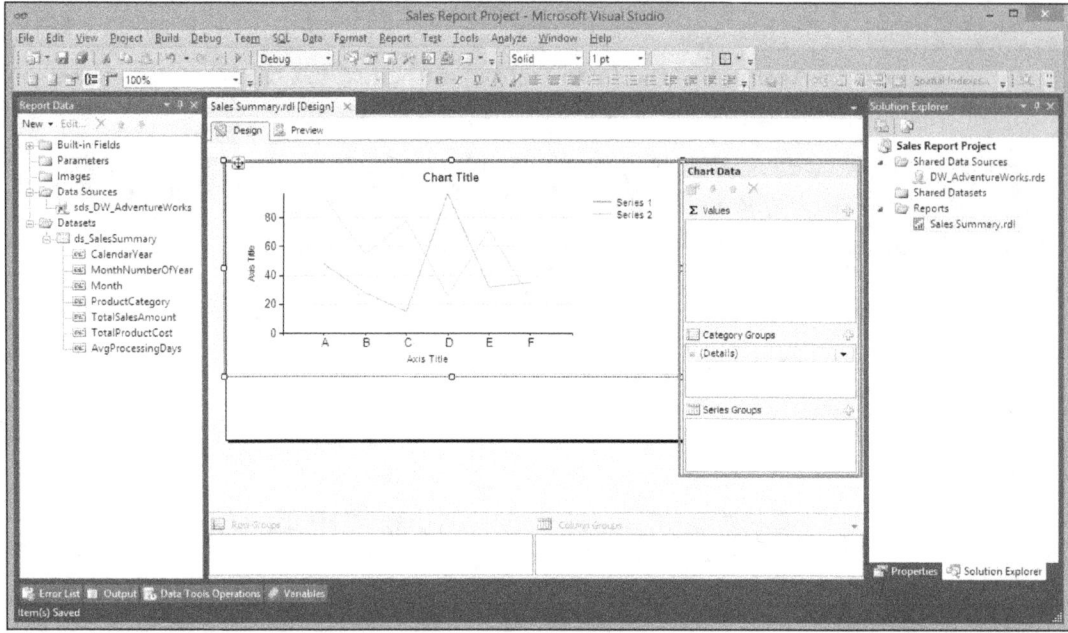

5. In the **Values** section of the **Chart Data** configuration box, click on the green button (shaped like a plus sign), and select the **TotalSalesAmount** data field from the options listed.

6. In the **Category Groups** section of the **Chart Data** configuration box, click on the drop-down arrow on the right-side of the **(Details)** item, and select the **Month** data field.

7. Click on the same drop-down arrow from the previous step, and select the **Category Group Properties…** option to bring up the **Category Group Properties** window as shown in the following screenshot:

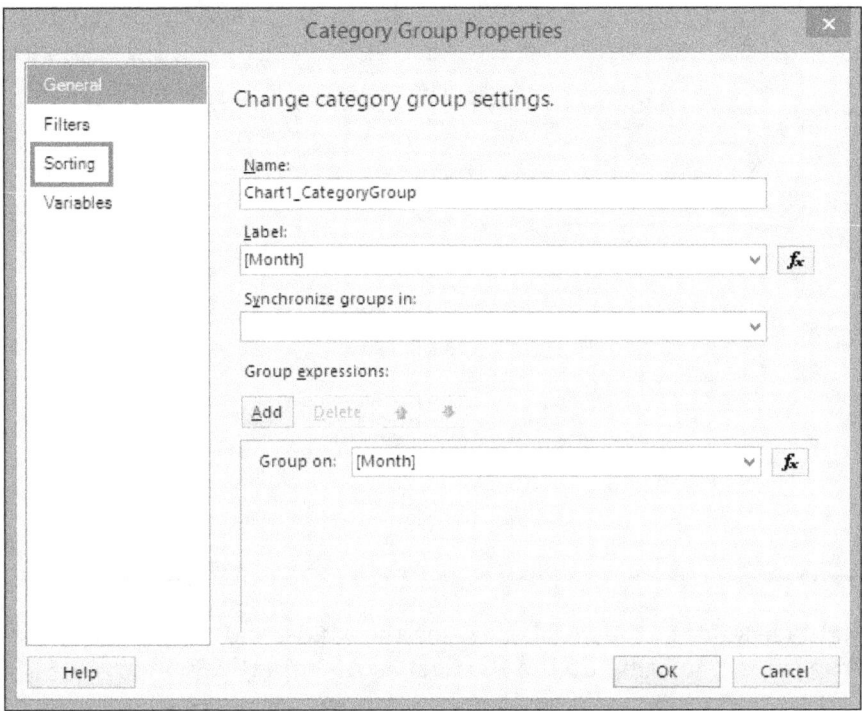

Category Group Properties dialog box

8. Select the **Sorting** tab, change the **Sort by** column from **[Month]** to **[MonthNumberOfYear]**, and click on **OK**. This will keep the months on the x axis sorted in the correct order; otherwise, they will be sorted alphabetically and data for August will appear before February, which is incorrect.

9. In the **Series Groups** section of the **Chart Data** configuration box, click on the green button (shaped like a plus sign), and select the **CalendarYear** data field from the options listed. This will separate the lines on the chart by year allowing the business users to compare year-over-year trends.

10. Right-click on the y axis label and uncheck the **Show Axis Title** option to remove it from the display.

11. Do the same with the x axis label.

12. Click on the chart title and change the title from **Chart Title** to **Year over Year – Sales Amount**.

13. The report should now resemble the one in the following screenshot:

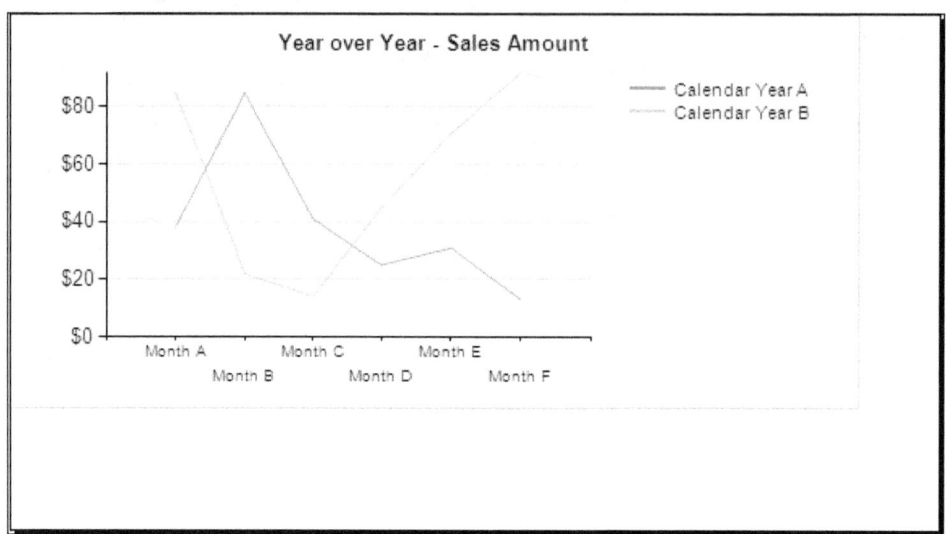

14. Right-click one of the numbers along the y axis, and select **Vertical Axis Properties...** to bring up the **Vertical Axis Properties** window.
15. In the **Number** tab, change the **Category** value from **Default** to **Currency**.
16. Change the number of decimal places from **2** to **0**, and select the checkbox **Use 1000 separator (,)**, as shown in the following screenshot:

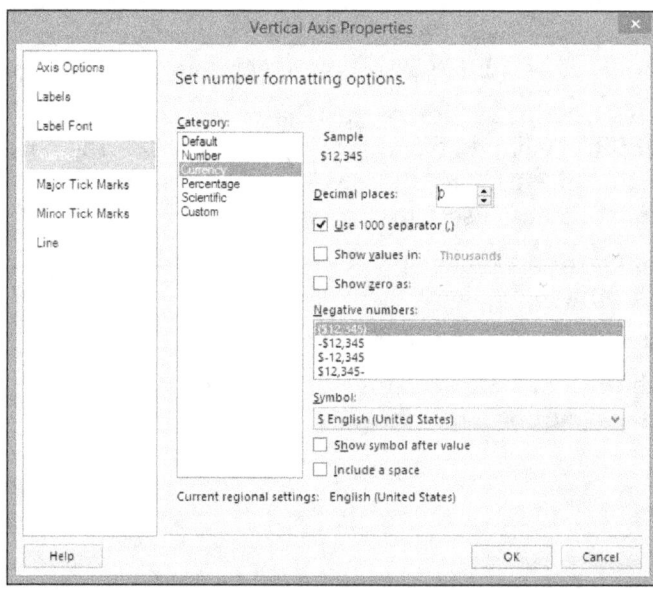

Number page of Vertical Axis Properties dialog box

17. Click on **OK** to save the changes.
18. Click on one of the months along the x axis, and select **Horizontal Axis Properties...** to bring up the **Horizontal Axis Properties** window.
19. In the **Axis Options** tab, change the value for **Interval** from **Auto** to **1** and click on **OK**. This will force every month value to be displayed on the x axis.
20. Right-click on a blank space in the chart and select **Chart Properties...** to bring up the **Chart Properties** window.
21. In the **Border** tab, click on the button above **None** in the **Presets** section and click on **OK** to remove the border from the chart.
22. At the top of the report canvas, click on the **Preview** tab (to the right of the **Design** tab) to run the report within SQL Server Data Tools. Your report should resemble the one in the following screenshot:

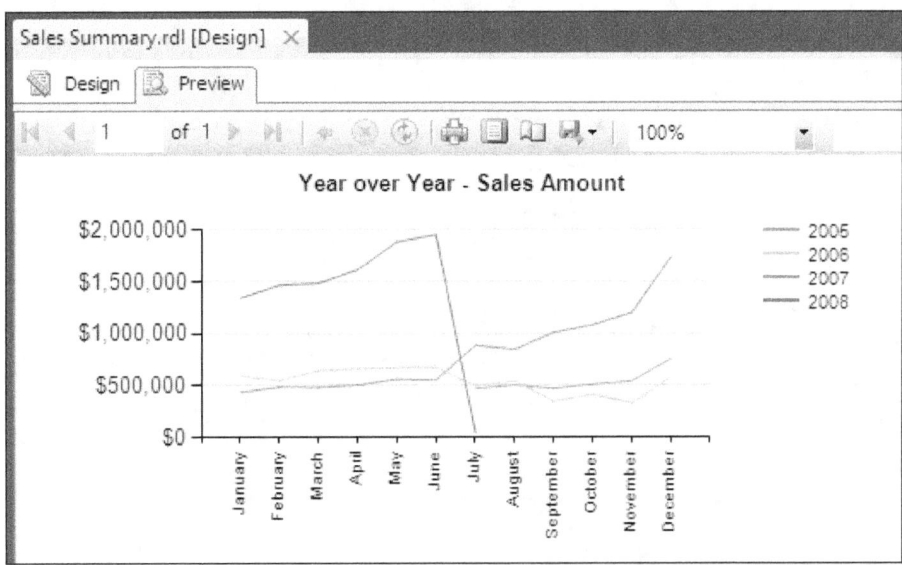

*Development Activity with SSRS*

## Deploying a report project

Now that the report has been developed and you are satisfied with the results in SSDT, it is time to deploy the report project. In this exercise, you will be deploying the report to a standalone report server installed in the Native mode. The process for deploying a report to a report server installed in SharePoint integrated mode is nearly identical; the only difference is the URLs used in the deployment configuration section of the **Report Server Project**.

1. In the **Solution Explorer** window (on the far right-hand side of the screen), right-click on the name of the project (for example, **Sales Report Project**), and select **Properties** to bring up the **Sales Report Project Property Pages** window, as shown in the following screenshot:

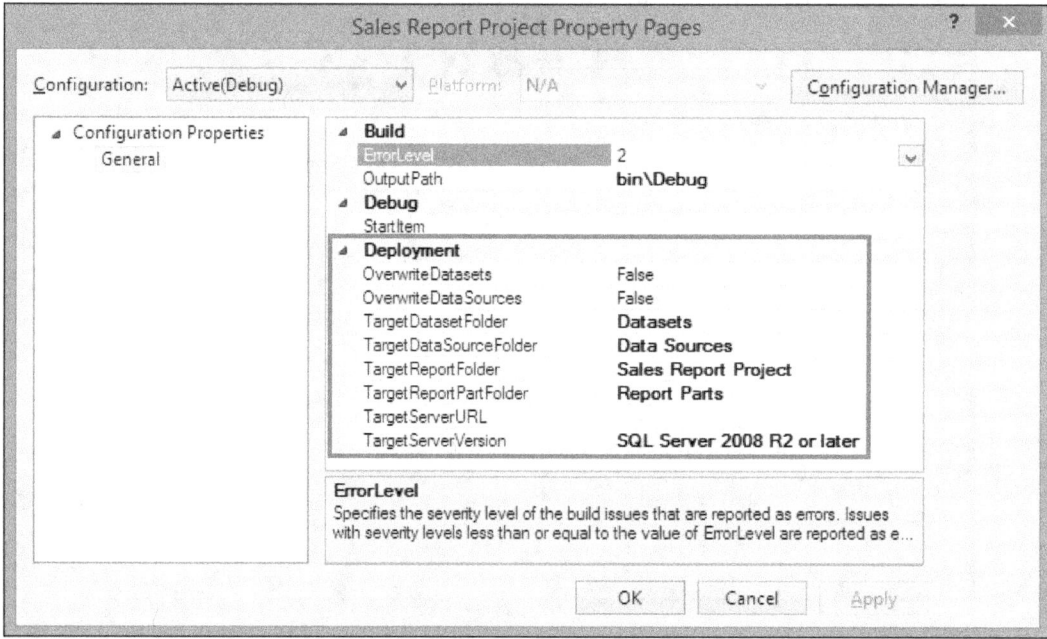

Sales Report Property Pages dialog box to configure deployment properties

2. The deployment section (shown in the preceding screenshot) contains several properties that control the deployment destination of the objects in the project. These properties are listed along with a brief description as follows:

    ◦ **OverwriteDatasets**: This property controls whether or not to overwrite the one already deployed if the project contains a shared dataset with the same name as one already deployed to the report server.

*Chapter 3*

- ° **OverwriteDataSources**: This property controls whether or not to overwrite the one already deployed if the project contains a shared data source with the same name as one already deployed to the report server.
- ° **TargetDatasetFolder**: This property controls the name of the folder where shared datasets contained in project will be deployed.
- ° **TargetDataSourceFolder**: This property controls the name of the folder where shared data sources contained in project will be deployed.
- ° **TargetReportFolder**: This property controls the name of the folder where report files contained in project will be deployed.
- ° **TargetReportPartFolder**: This property controls the name of the folder where shared report parts contained in project will be deployed.

>  For all of the previous properties defining folder locations, if the folder does not already exist, a new one will be created.

- ° **TargetServerURL**: This property contains the URL of the report server and servers as the base path for all of the **\*Folder** properties listed earlier. While deploying to a report server installed in the SharePoint Integrated mode, this URL will point to the SharePoint site.
- ° **TargetServerVersion**: This property contains the version of the report server to which the project will be deployed. While deploying to SQL Server Reporting Services 2012, leave this value at SQL Server 2008 R2 or later.

3. Enter the appropriate value for the **TargetServerURL** property and leave all other deployment properties set to the defaults. In my case, with a default report server installation on the same system that I have used to develop this report, I can simply use the URL `http://localhost/ReportServer`.

4. After clicking on **OK** to save the changes to the project properties, right-click on the name of the project (for example, **Sales Report Project**) in the **Solution Explorer** window, and select **Deploy** to deploy all objects in the project to the report server.

5. Now business users can open up a browser and navigate to the report server, where they should see the items that were just deployed (shown in the following screenshot). The shared data source can be found in the `Data Sources` folder, while the report, **Sales Summary**, can be found in the `Sales Report Project` folder.

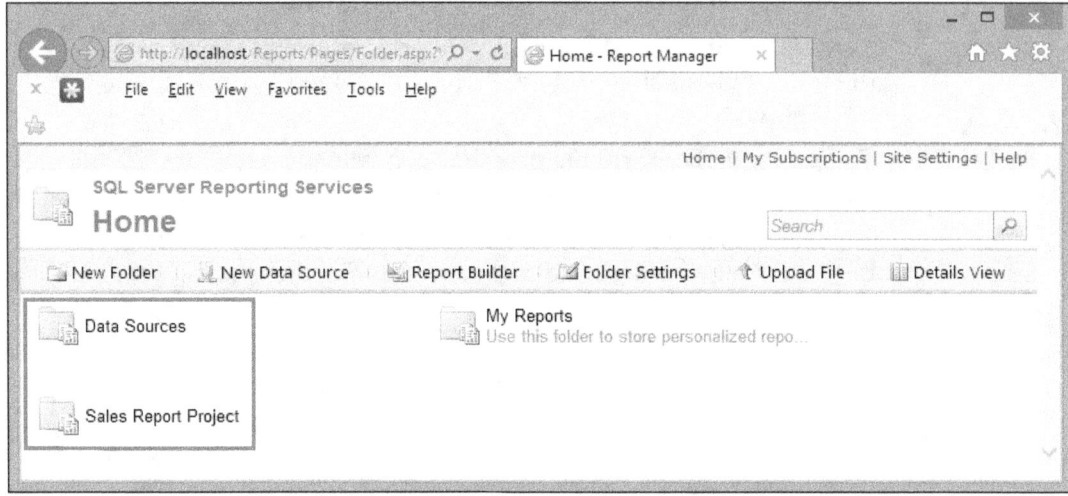

Report Server showing new folders created during the deployment process

# Summary

In this chapter, we stepped into the shoes of a report developer and created a Reporting Services report from start to finish using SQL Server Data Tools. Readers should now be familiar with creating a SQL Server report project consisting of a shared data source and report with a line chart and then deploying it to a standalone report server installed in the Native mode.

In the next chapter, we will switch gears and learn about Power View, a new self-service reporting tool geared more towards business users who wish to create their own reports.

# 4
# Power View – Self-service Reporting

Self-service reporting is when business users have the ability to create personalized reports and analytical queries without requiring the IT department to get involved.

There will be some basic work that the IT department must do, namely creating the various data marts that the reporting tools will use as well as deploying those reporting tools. However, once that is done, IT will be freed of creating reports so that they can work on other tasks. Instead, the people who know the data best—the business users—will be able to build the reports.

Here is a typical scenario that occurs when a self-service reporting solution is not in place: a business user wants a report created, so they fill out a report request that gets routed to IT. The IT department is backlogged with report requests, so it takes them weeks to get back to the user. When they do, they interview the user to get more details about exactly what data the user wants on the report and the look of the report (the business requirements). The IT person may not know the data that well, so they will have to get educated by the user on what the data means. This leads to mistakes in understanding what the user is requesting. The IT person may take away an incorrect assumption of what data the report should contain or how it should look. Then, the IT person goes back and creates the report. A week or so goes by and he shows the user the report. Then, they hear things from the user such as "that is not correct" or "that is not what I meant". The IT person fixes the report and presents it to the user once again. More problems are noticed, fixes are made, and this cycle is repeated four to five times before the report is finally up to the user's satisfaction. In the end, a lot of time has been wasted by the business user and the IT person, and the finished version of the report took way longer that it should have.

This is where a self-service reporting tool such as **Power View** comes in. It is so intuitive and easy to use that most business users can start developing reports with it with little or no training. The interface is so visually appealing that it makes report writing fun. This results in users creating their own reports, thereby empowering businesses to make timely, proactive decisions and explore issues much more effectively than ever before.

In this chapter, we will cover the major features and functions of Power View, including the setup, various ways to start Power View, data visualizations, the user interface, data models, deploying and sharing reports, multiple views, chart highlighting, slicing, filters, sorting, exporting to PowerPoint, and finally, design tips. We will also talk about PowerPivot and the **Business Intelligence Sematic Model (BISM)**. By the end of the chapter, you should be able to jump right in and start creating reports.

# Getting started

**Power View** was first introduced as a new integrated reporting feature of SQL Server 2012 (Enterprise or BI Edition) with SharePoint 2010 Enterprise Edition. It has also been seamlessly integrated and built directly into Excel 2013 and made available as an add-in that you can simply enable (although it is not possible to share Power View reports between SharePoint and Excel).

Power View allows users to quickly create highly visual and interactive reports via a **What You See Is What You Get (WYSIWYG)** interface. The following screenshot gives an example of a type of report you can build with Power View, which includes various types of visualizations:

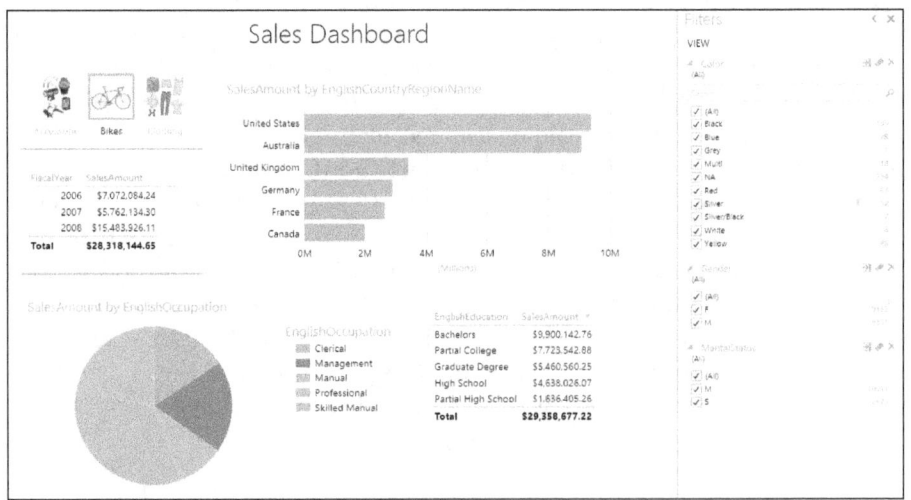

Sales Dashboard

The following screenshot is another example of a Power View report that makes heavy use of slicers along with a bar chart and tables:

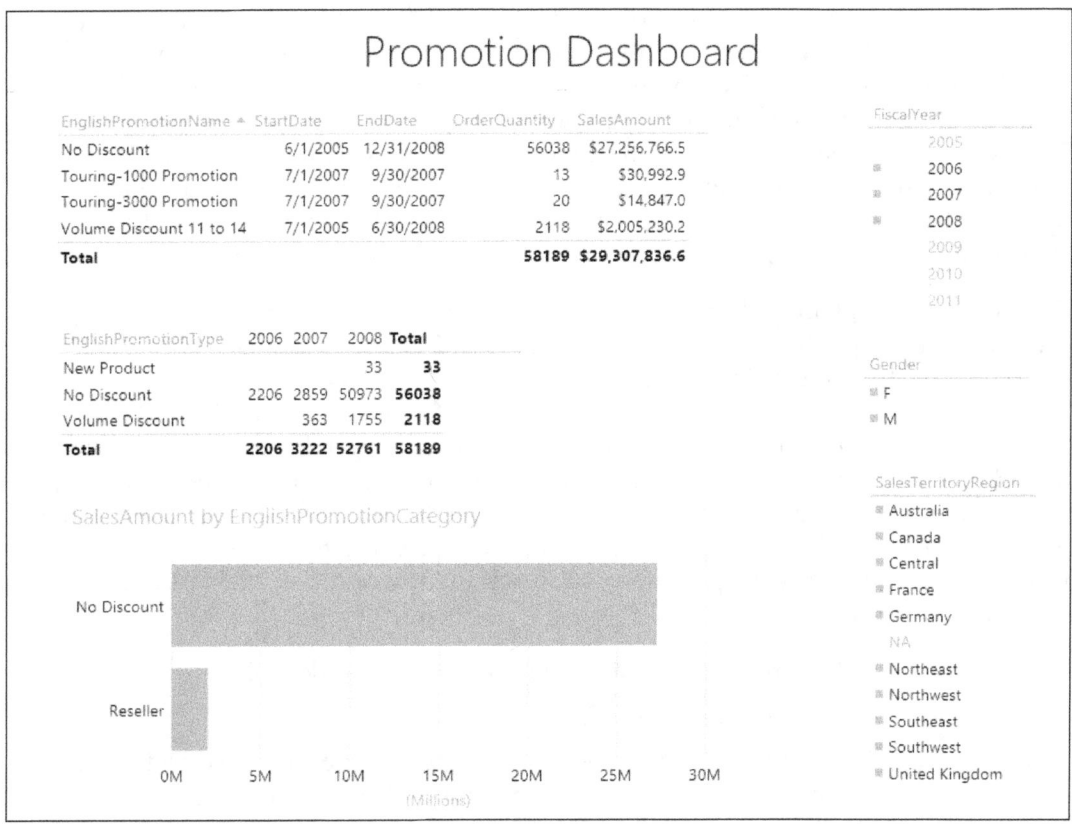

Promotion Dashboard

We will start by discussing PowerPivot and BISM and will then go over the setup procedures for the two possible ways to use Power View: through SharePoint or via Excel 2013.

# PowerPivot

It is important to understand what PowerPivot is and how it relates to Power View. PowerPivot is a data analysis add-on for Microsoft Excel. With it, you can mash large amounts of data together that you can then analyze and aggregate all in one workbook, bypassing the Excel maximum worksheet size of one million rows. It uses a powerful data engine to analyze and query large volumes of data very quickly. There are many data sources that you can use to import data into PowerPivot. Once the data is imported, it becomes part of a data model, which is simply a collection of tables that have relationships between them. Since the data is in Excel, it is immediately available to PivotTables, PivotCharts, and Power View.

PowerPivot is implemented in an application window separate from Excel that gives you the ability to do such things as insert and delete columns, format text, hide columns from client tools, change column names, and add images. Once you complete your changes, you have the option of uploading (publishing) the PowerPivot workbook to a PowerPivot Gallery or document library (on a BI site) in SharePoint (a PowerPivot Gallery is a special type of SharePoint document library that provides document and preview management for published Excel workbooks that contain PowerPivot data). This will allow you to share the data model inside PowerPivot with others. To publish your PowerPivot workbook to SharePoint, perform the following steps:

1. Open the Excel file that contains the PowerPivot workbook.
2. Select the **File** tab on the ribbon.
3. If using Excel 2013, click on **Save As** and then click on **Browse** and enter the SharePoint location of the PowerPivot Gallery (see the next screenshot).

   If using Excel 2010, click on **Save & Send**, click on **Save to SharePoint**, and then click on **Browse**.
4. Click on **Save** and the file will then be uploaded to SharePoint and immediately be made available to others.

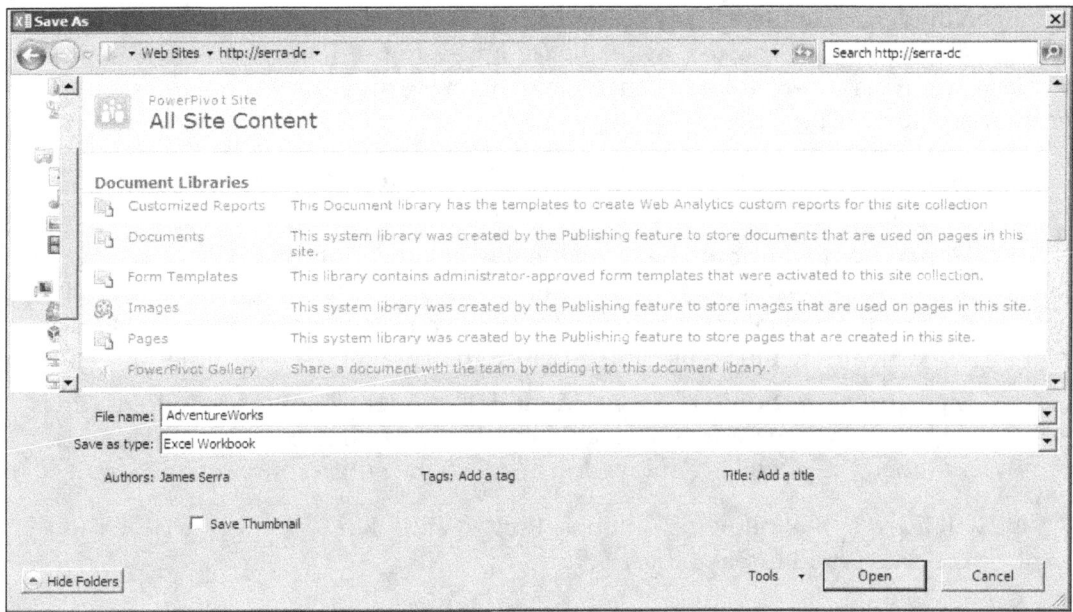

Saving files to the PowerPivot Gallery

A Power View report can be built from the PowerPivot workbook in the PowerPivot Gallery in SharePoint or from the PowerPivot workbook in an Excel 2013 file.

# Business Intelligence Semantic Model

**Business Intelligence Semantic Model (BISM)** is a new data model that was introduced by Microsoft in SQL Server 2012. It is a single unified BI platform that publicizes one model for all end-user experiences. It is a hybrid model that exposes two storage implementations: the multidimensional data model (formerly called OLAP) and the tabular data model, which uses the xVelocity engine (formally called VertiPaq), all of which are hosted in **SQL Server Analysis Services (SSAS)**.

The tabular data model provides the architecture and optimization in a format that is the same as the data storage method used by PowerPivot, which uses an in-memory analytics engine to deliver fast access to tabular data. Tabular data models are built using **SQL Server Data Tools (SSDT)** and can be created from scratch or by importing a PowerPivot data model contained within an Excel workbook.

Once the model is complete, it is deployed to an SSAS server instance configured for tabular storage mode to make it available for others to use. This provides a great way to create a self-service BI solution, then make it a department solution and then an enterprise solution, as shown:

- **Self-service solution**: A business user loads data into PowerPivot and analyzes the data, making improvements along the way.
- **Department solution**: The Excel file that contains the PowerPivot workbook is deployed to a SharePoint site used by the department (in which the active data model actually resides in an SSAS instance and not in the Excel file). Department members use and enhance the data model over time.
- **Enterprise solution**: The PowerPivot data model from the SharePoint site is imported into a tabular data model by the IT department. Security is added and then the model is deployed to SSAS so the entire company can use it.

As we will learn in the following sections, Power View can be used to analyze and explore the data for all three of these solutions.

# Power View within SharePoint

This section describes using Power View within SharePoint. It can be used with the enterprise editions of SharePoint 2010 or SharePoint 2013.

# Setup

Although Power View is very easy to use, setting up the required infrastructure when using it with SharePoint can be a bit tricky. Power View is automatically installed when you run the SQL Server 2012 setup and choose **Reporting Services Add-in for SharePoint Products** on the **Feature Selection** page. This is a newer version of the add-in, which includes Power View, compared to the version that is installed with SharePoint 2010 that does not include Power View. The following are the software requirements for Power View:

- SQL Server 2012 database engine (Business Intelligence Edition or Enterprise Edition).
- SQL Server 2012 Reporting Services (in SharePoint Integrated mode).
- SQL Server 2012 PowerPivot for SharePoint.
- SQL Server 2012 Analysis Services (SSAS) in tabular mode if using a tabular model connection.

- SQL Server 2012 Analysis Services in multidimensional mode if using a multidimensional model connection. It requires that SQL Server 2012 Service Pack 1 Cumulative Update 4 (CU4) be applied.
- SQL Server 2008/2012 Analysis Services in PowerPivot for SharePoint mode if using a PowerPivot for SharePoint workbook.
- SharePoint Server 2010/2013 Enterprise Edition **Reporting Services Add-in for SharePoint Products** installed from SQL Server 2012 onto the SharePoint server on which you want to have Power View.
- Microsoft Silverlight 5.

> Providing detailed instructions for installing all the software to support Power View is outside the scope of this book. For help with this, see the Microsoft white paper titled *Power View Infrastructure Configuration and Installation: Step-by-Step and Scripts*, which walks you through installing and testing Power View and its infrastructure using multiple scenarios: http://bit.ly/1bqaSZT.

The data sources that Power View in SharePoint can use are a tabular model connection or a multidimensional model connection (support for multidimensional models was added after SQL Server 2012 was released via SP1 CU4).

## Tabular model connection

The tabular model connection can be implemented in a number of ways:

- It can be a PowerPivot workbook (.xlsx) that is published to a SharePoint site that has PowerPivot enabled (called PowerPivot for SharePoint). Once published, the data is actually saved to a SharePoint PowerPivot flavor of the tabular engine. You can then use a special-purpose document library called PowerPivot Gallery to preview, share, and access published workbooks.
- It can be a BISM report server data source (.rsds) type that is published in a SharePoint document library in which it connects to a database running on a SQL Server 2012 Analysis Services tabular mode server (which can use either Windows authentication or stored credentials as Windows credentials).

- It can be a BISM connection file (.bism) that is published in a SharePoint library (which has the BISM connection file content type) in which the connection is pointing to either one of the following:

    - A database running on a SQL Server 2012 Analysis Services tabular mode server (which can use only Windows authentication and not stored credentials).
    - A PowerPivot for SharePoint workbook. Note that an embedded PowerPivot database inside an Excel workbook is the equivalent of a tabular model database that is run on a standalone Analysis Services tabular mode server. You can use workbooks that are created using either the SQL Server 2008 R2 or the Microsoft SQL Server 2012 versions of PowerPivot for Excel.

You can also open the previously mentioned BISM connection file in Excel as an ODBC file. If you do this, Excel will open a workbook that contains a PivotTable field list that is populated with fields from the underlying data source.

PowerPivot for SharePoint requires Excel Services and also requires that you install SQL Server PowerPivot for SharePoint (which installs the "PowerPivot for SharePoint" server mode in SSAS). A benefit when using the tabular model is that a PowerPivot for SharePoint model workbook is able to use many different data sources, such as Microsoft Access, SQL Server 2008, SQL Azure, multidimensional databases, Excel files, text files, and so on. When using one of these sources, a SSAS tabular cube is created behind the scenes. So, the tabular model acts as a bridge, or a semantic layer, between the complexities of the data sources at the backend and your perspective of the data.

Be aware that when the tabular model connection uses a PowerPivot for SharePoint workbook, you are using the saved data in that workbook and are not connected to the source of that data. For example, if you are using a Microsoft Access database as a source for PowerPivot, when you save the PowerPivot workbook to SharePoint, you in fact are using a static copy of the data from the Microsoft Access database that was imported into PowerPivot. Then, when you are using Power View connected to this PowerPivot for SharePoint workbook, you are using that static data and are not connecting to the Microsoft Access database until you refresh the PowerPivot model either manually or using a scheduled refresh.

# Starting Power View connected to a tabular model connection

If you would like to use the first tabular model connection discussed earlier to start Power View, you would first use PowerPivot in Excel to pull in the data and then save the PowerPivot workbook to the PowerPivot Gallery in SharePoint. Then, you would go to the PowerPivot Gallery in SharePoint. Just to the right of the name of the PowerPivot workbook will be a **Create Power View Report** control. Click on that, and you will be able to create a Power View report from the PowerPivot model in the workbook. See the following screenshot on how to start Power View in PowerPivot Gallery:

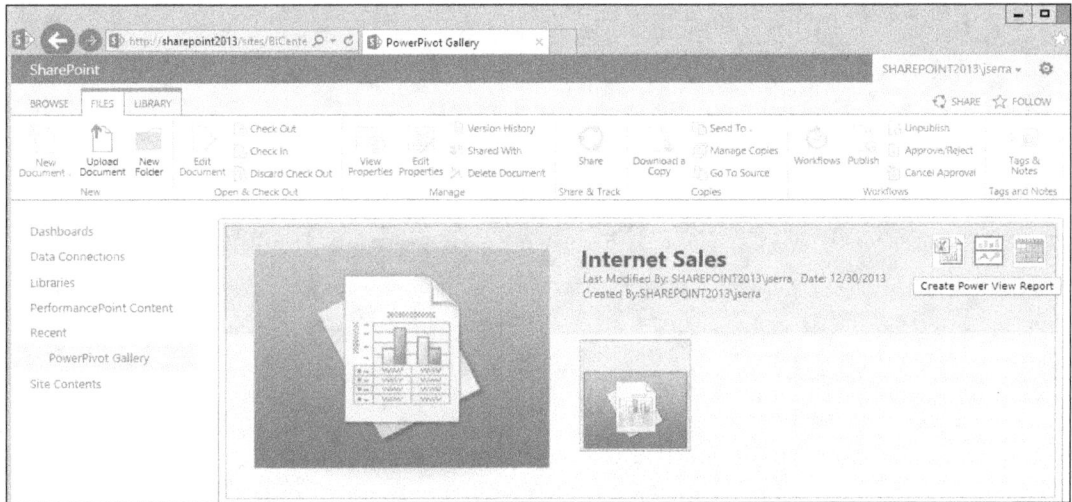

Starting Power View in PowerPivot Gallery

To start Power View using the other tabular model connections discussed earlier, just click on the connection in the library or open the connections context menu and you will see the option **Create Power View report**.

## Multidimensional model connection

The multidimensional model connection is made by creating a BISM report server data source (.rsds) type that is published in a SharePoint document library. This data source connects to a database running on a SQL Server 2012 Analysis Services multidimensional mode server (which can use either Windows authentication or stored credentials as Windows credentials). See the following screenshot to see what your BISM report server data source connection should look like:

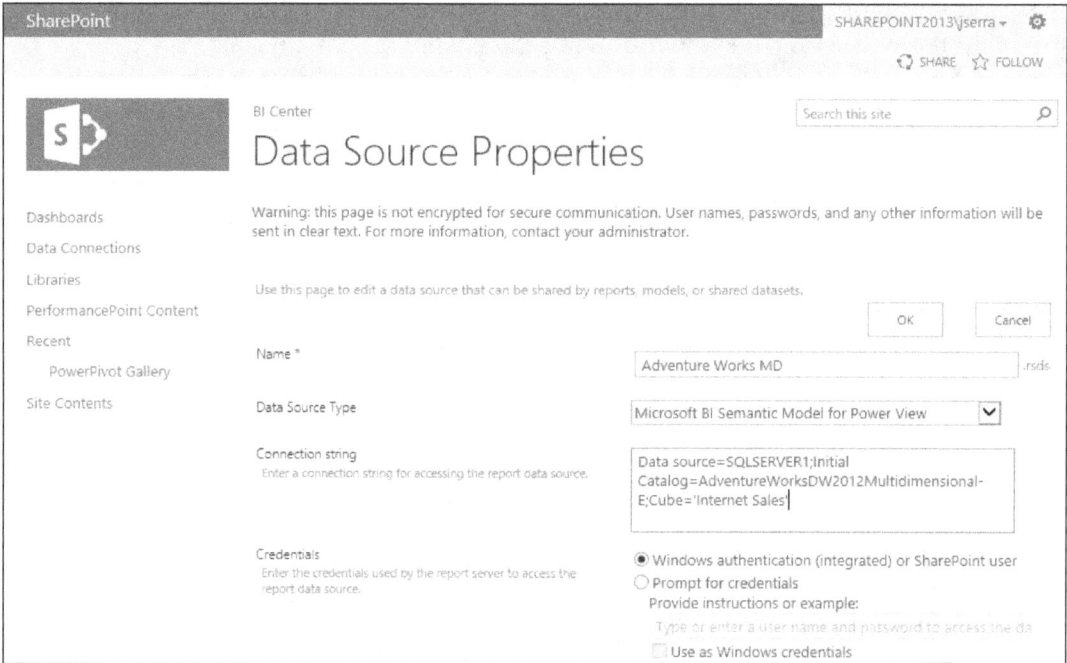

BISM report server data source connection

## Starting Power View connected to a multidimensional model connection

To start Power View with a multidimensional model connection, in the SharePoint document library, either click on the connection to the multidimensional model or open the multidimensional models context menu and you will see the option **Create Power View report**.

It is important to understand that when you create a Power View report using the multidimensional model, you are working with a tabular model type representation of a multidimensional model. Some objects and behaviors may appear different from the traditional tabular models. For more information on the differences, see http://bit.ly/1djQlt4.

## Power View within Excel 2013

This section describes using Power View within Excel 2013, which requires the ProPlus Edition of Office 2013. Note that Power View is not supported within Excel 2010 or earlier versions.

## Setup

Power View is an add-on in Excel 2013 that you can enable by following these steps:

1. In Excel, navigate to **FILE** | **Options** | **Add-Ins**.
2. In the **Manage** box, click on the drop-down arrow and select **COM Add-ins**. Now, click on **Go**.
3. Check the **Power View** checkbox and click on **OK**.

If the Power View add-on has not been enabled, it will be grayed out on the Excel **Insert** menu.

## Data models

Excel 2013 (ProPlus Edition) now has native support for data models. A data model is a brand new approach to integrating data from multiple tables, in essence, building a relational data source right inside an Excel workbook. The data models are used transparently to provide the tabular data used in a Power View report.

When importing relational data, a data model will be created implicitly when you select multiple tables. The source of this data can be any relational database, such as SQL Server, SQL Azure, or Microsoft Access. A data model can contain a single table if you choose to add the data to the data model when importing the data, as depicted in the following screenshot. These are internal data models that you can view in PowerPivot.

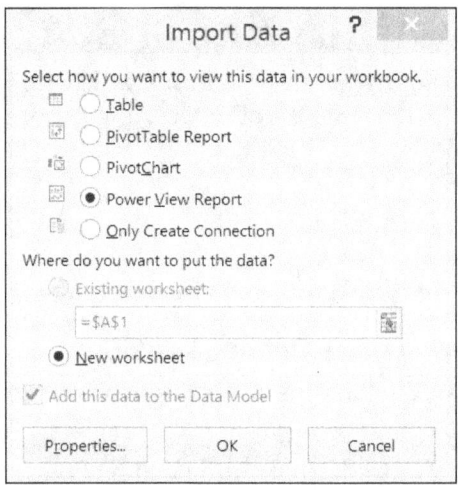

The Import Data dialog

In addition, Power View can also use an external data model from an external data source, such as other PowerPivot workbooks or SSAS tabular models, which will provide you with more functionality than using data models. Multidimensional models are not supported in Excel.

## Starting Power View in Excel

To start Power View, when importing data, choose to view the data in your workbook as a **Power View Report** (as shown in the preceding screenshot), or in Excel, go to the **INSERT** ribbon and click on **Power View**. If starting Power View from the **INSERT** ribbon, you must have some data on an existing sheet for it to use (this can be data you imported or simply typed in).

## Importing data into Excel

There are numerous ways to import data into Excel and then have that data consumed by Power View. Here are the four most common ways.

## Adding data to a worksheet and inserting data into Power View

Follow these steps:

1. While in a blank workbook in Excel, go to the **DATA** tab and use one of the options in the **Get External Data** group.
2. Eventually, you will reach an **Import Data** dialog. Select **Table** and leave **Add this data to the Data Model** unchecked. This will add the data to a worksheet.
3. Select the range of cells that contain data that you want to use in your Power View report. Then, go to the **INSERT** tab and choose **Power View**.
4. The data will then be displayed in Power View, and in the **Power View Fields** section, you will see **Range** as the table name with a database icon.
5. The database icon indicates that data is being imported from a worksheet. If the data is changed in the worksheet, you can click **Refresh** in Power View (and also in PowerPivot) to pull in the updated data.
6. Behind the scenes, it adds the data to a PowerPivot data model with the name **Range**.

## Not adding data to a worksheet and inserting data into Power View

Follow these steps:

1. While in a blank workbook in Excel, go to the **DATA** tab and use one of the options in the **Get External Data** group.
2. Eventually, you will reach an **Import Data** dialog. Check **Add this data to the Data Model** and **Power View Report** (**Power View Report** requires the **Add this data to the Data Model** box to be checked). This does not add data to a worksheet.
3. A blank Power View report will be displayed, and in the Power View **Fields** section, you will see the table name (derived based on the name of the source) without a database icon. A missing database icon means there is no data in a worksheet.
4. Behind the scenes, the data is added to a PowerPivot data model with the same name as the table name in the **Power View Fields** section.

## Adding data to a worksheet and using PowerPivot

Follow these steps:

1. While in a blank workbook in Excel, go to the **DATA** tab and use one of the options in the **Get External Data** group.

2. Eventually, you will reach an **Import Data** dialog. Select **Table** and leave the **Add this data to the Data Model** box unchecked. This will add the data to a worksheet. Or, instead of getting external data, you can type your own data into the worksheet.

3. Go to the **PowerPivot** tab, choose **Add to Data Model**, and select the range of cells that contain data that you want to use in your Power View report. This changes the selected data on the worksheet into a table and adds it to the PowerPivot data model with the name **Table1**.

4. Go to the **INSERT** tab and choose **Power View**. The data will then be displayed in Power View, and in the **Power View Fields** section, you will see **Table1** as the table name with a database icon.

> If you get the error **A table cannot overlap a range that contains a PivotTable report, query results, protected cells or another table** when choosing **Add to Data Model**, go to **DATA | Properties** and uncheck **Save query definition**. This is because when you imported the data, you created an external data range (also called a query table) and need to remove the query definition from the sheet to allow it to be added to PowerPivot.

## Not adding data to a worksheet and using PowerPivot

Follow these steps:

1. While in a blank workbook in Excel, open PowerPivot by going to the **PowerPivot** tab and choosing **Manage**.

2. Import data via the **Get External Data** option in PowerPivot. This adds the data to the PowerPivot data model and gives it a name based on the name of the source.

3. Go to the **INSERT** tab and choose **Power View**. Then, a blank Power View report will be displayed. In the **Power View Fields** section, you will see the table name without a database icon that is the same name as the Power View data model. This does not add data to a worksheet.

 You cannot edit data in PowerPivot; you can only update the data from the source by using the **Refresh** button.

If you make a change to the data model in PowerPivot, when you return to Power View, you will get this message: **The Data Model has changed. When you finish editing the Data Model, click OK to apply these changes in Power View**. The data model changes are then applied immediately.

## Data visualizations

Before getting into how to create a report in Power View, it is a good idea to go over the types of reports that you can create. The following table describes the different charts and visualizations that are available to you in Power View to create reports. For examples of what each chart looks like, check out http://bit.ly/NKFmTd.

| Visualization | Description |
|---|---|
| Table | A table is simply made up of rows and columns. For each visualization that you want to create, you will start first with creating a table. Then you can convert the table to any other visualizations. |
| Matrix | A matrix is similar to a table, but it can be collapsed and expanded by rows and/or columns. It can display totals and subtotals by row and column and can drill up and down a hierarchy. |
| Card | A card provides an index card style layout that includes text and data values as well as images. |
| Stacked Bar Chart | Categories are usually organized along the vertical axis and with values along the horizontal axis. A stacked bar chart shows the relationship of individual items to the whole. |
| 100% Stacked Bar Chart | Categories are usually organized along the vertical axis and with values along the horizontal axis. This compares the percentage that each value contributes to a total across categories. |
| Clustered Bar Chart | Categories are usually organized along the vertical axis and with values along the horizontal axis. The compares values across categories. |
| Stacked Column Chart | Categories are usually organized along the horizontal axis and with values along the vertical axis. This shows the relationship of individual items to the whole. |

| Visualization | Description |
| --- | --- |
| 100% Stacked Column Chart | Categories are usually organized along the horizontal axis and with values along the vertical axis. This compares the percentage that each value contributes to a total across categories. |
| Clustered Column Chart | Categories are usually organized along the horizontal axis and with values along the vertical axis. This compares values across categories. |
| Scatter Chart | The horizontal axis displays one numeric field and the vertical axis displays another, which makes it easy to see the relationship that exists between the two values for all items in the chart. It provides a play button feature to enable viewing how data changes over time. It is also called bubble chart. |
| Line Chart | It has only one value axis (called the vertical axis), and the horizontal axis only shows evenly spaced groupings, or categories, of data. Category data is spread evenly along a category (horizontal) axis and distributes all numerical value data along a value (vertical) axis. |
| Pie Chart | This is a circular chart divided into sectors that illustrate numerical proportion. Pie charts can be rather sophisticated by allowing you to drill down when you double-click on a slice, or they can show sub-slices within the larger color slices. It also has the ability to cross-filter a pie chart with another chart. |
| Map | Map displays your data in the context of geography using Bing map files. You can zoom as well as pan just as you would with any other Bing map. The data is plotted using geographical elements such as latitude and longitude. |
| Tiles | Tiles convert a matrix or table to present tabular data interactively. There will be a dynamic navigation strip that uses text or images for each tile. Clicking on a tile filters the data. |
| Multiples | This creates a series of charts that have identical x and y axes and arrange them side by side to make it easy to compare different values at the same time. They are also called trellis charts. |

# The user interface

Once you start Power View, the interface you will see will be a bit different depending on whether you are using Power View through SharePoint or Excel.

Power View through SharePoint looks like this:

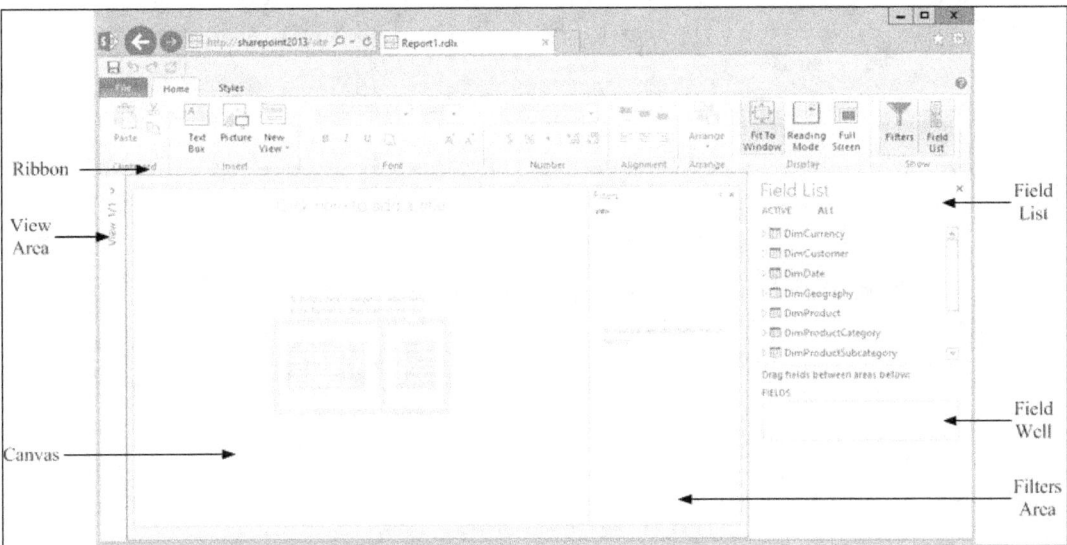

Power View in SharePoint

Power View through Excel looks like this:

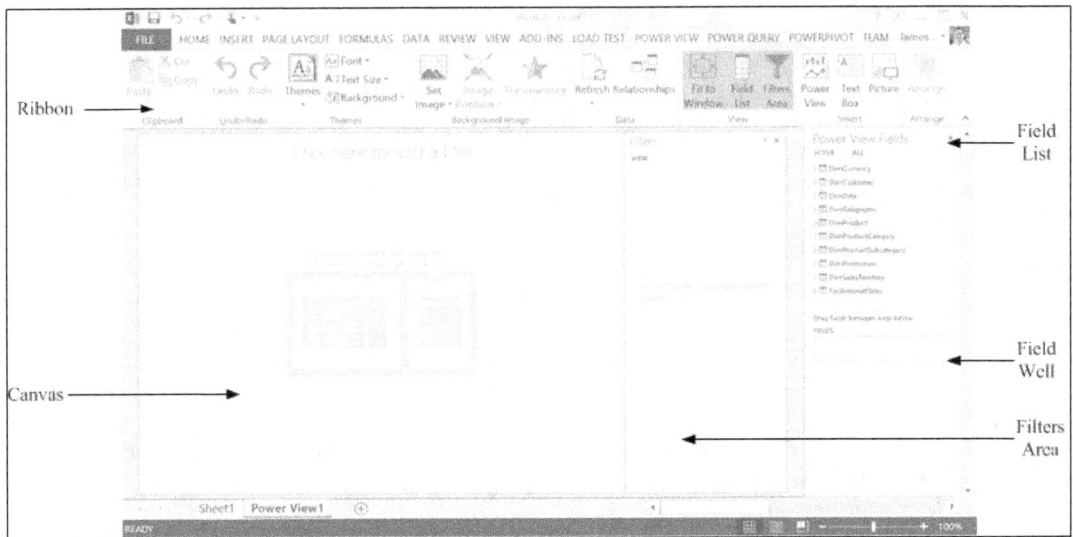

Power View in Excel 2013

Note that in SharePoint there is a **View Area**, while in Excel there isn't one. The biggest difference is with the ribbons. In Excel, there are three ribbons that are used exclusively by Power View. The Power View ribbon is always visible, as shown in the following screenshot:

The Power View ribbon in Excel 2013

The Design ribbon, as shown in the following screenshot, is visible when a visualization is selected:

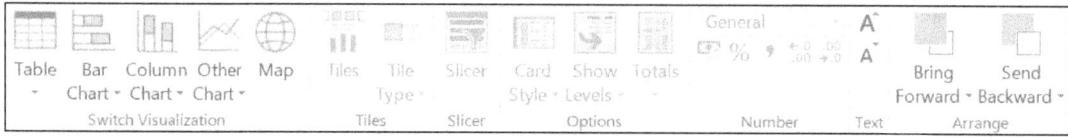

The Design ribbon in Excel 2013

The Layout ribbon, as shown in the screenshot, is visible when a chart is selected:

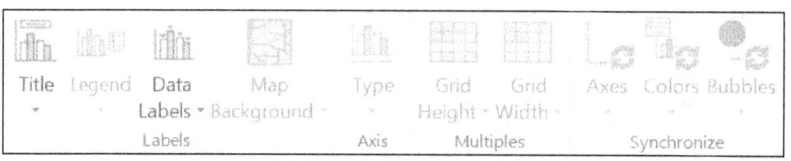

The Layout ribbon in Excel 2013

In SharePoint, you have the Home ribbon, which is always visible, as shown in the following screenshot:

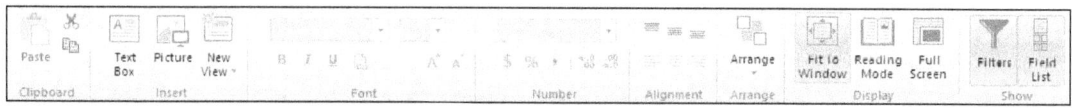

The Home ribbon in SharePoint

The Styles ribbon, as shown in the following screenshot, is always visible (the selected theme will change the colors for the entire view):

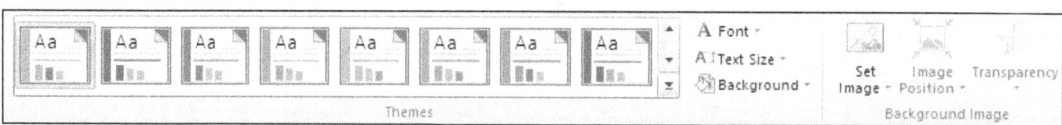

The Styles ribbon in SharePoint

The Design ribbon is visible when a visualization is selected:

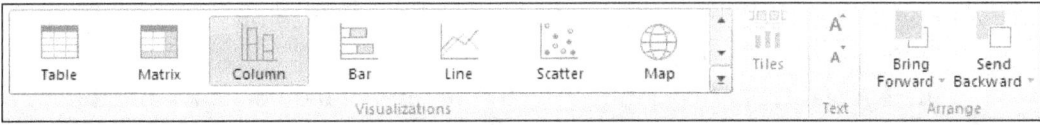

The Design ribbon in SharePoint

The Layout ribbon is visible when a chart is selected. It will have different buttons depending whether you are on a chart, as shown in the following screenshot:

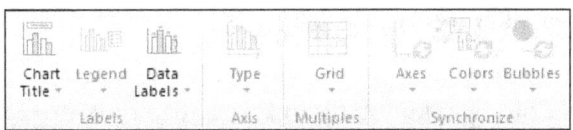

The Layout ribbon for charts in SharePoint

The Layout ribbon is visible when a map is selected, as shown in the following screenshot:

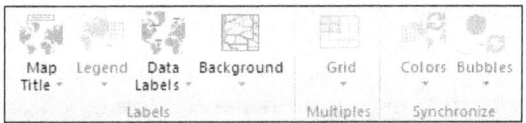

The Layout ribbon for map in SharePoint

The parts of the interface are described as follows:

- **Ribbon**: This is located at the top. It contains all the commands that can be performed either on the entire report or on the currently selected object in the report. Common tasks are grouped together.

- **View Area**: This is available only in SharePoint. It is located on the left-hand side. It tracks different states or views of the data in order to analyze the data at various points in time or as values change.

- **Canvas**: The center section is what contains the different data visualizations in the report. This is where you place the tables, charts, and filters that will display selected data from the data sources.

- **Field List**: This is on the upper right of the screen and contains the tables and fields from the data model. You will move these fields to build the report.

- **Field Well**: This is located in the bottom-right corner and is where you drag fields from the field list and drop them so they appear on the canvas. It also provides the properties of any object currently selected on the canvas so that you can control the appearance and behavior.
- **Filters Area**: This is used to restrict the amount of data displayed in the canvas area. It can be minimized by clicking on the **>** toggle at the top of the filters area or hidden completely by clicking on the **Filters Area** button on the ribbon.

# Enhancing data models

As mentioned in the previous sections, possible data sources for Power View are a PowerPivot for SharePoint workbook or an Excel 2013 data model. Both allow you to view and edit the data models in PowerPivot while in Excel. A benefit is that it allows you to make enhancements to the data model before users start to create reports against it in Power View. The enhancements can also be made to a tabular model via a Tabular Analysis Services project in **SQL Server Data Tools (SSDT)**.

The following are some of the enhancements you can make:

- **Default Field Set**: This setting is used for a table and gives you the ability to select default columns and measures and define the preferred order. Then, these columns and measures are automatically added to the Power View report canvas when you create a report and click on the table name displayed in the field list in Power View. This will help to reduce redundant steps when using a data model in a report. To set the default fields for a data model, go to a PowerPivot window and on the **Advanced** tab, there is a **Reporting Properties** section with a **Default Field Set** button. Click on this button and you will see the **Default Field Set** dialog box (see the following screenshot). To set the default fields for a tabular model, in SSDT, go to the properties of the appropriate table, and in the **Default Field Set** property, click on **Click to edit**.

*Chapter 4*

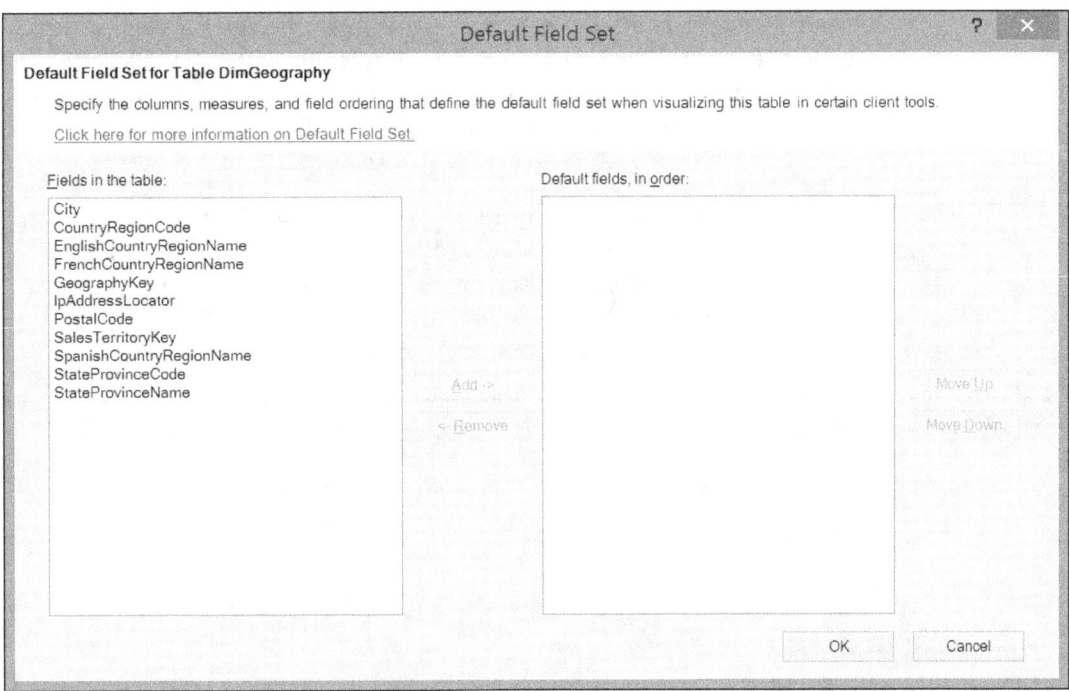

Default Field Set dialog box

- **Table Behavior**: There are numerous properties that can be set to control the behavior for a particular table:
    - **Row Identifier**: This is used to determine which column in the table is the primary key (unique identifier); this column must not have any blank values.
    - **Keep Unique Rows**: This lets you define which column or columns in the table should be used to establish unique rows when reporting, even if the column or columns have duplicates. For example, if two customers have the same first and last name, choose the first and last name fields for **Keep Unique Rows** so that they are treated as two distinct customers instead of being grouped together.
    - **Default Label**: This allows you to provide a display name for each unique row in the table. For example, you can specify a customer's name as the display name for a customer record. Power View reports such as tiles that use labels will emphasize this display name on the report (for example, use a bigger font for the display name).

*Power View – Self-service Reporting*

- **Default Image**: This allows you to provide an image for each unique row in the table. The default image can refer to text columns that provide URL references to image files, or it can reference binary data-type columns. Power View reports, such as tiles that use images, will emphasize the image on the report (for example, use a larger image).

To set the table behavior for a data model, go to a PowerPivot window, and on the **Advanced** tab, there is a **Reporting Properties** section with a **Table Behavior** button (see the following screenshot). To set the table behavior for a tabular model, in SSDT, go to the properties of the appropriate table, and in the **Table Behavior** property, click on **Click to edit**.

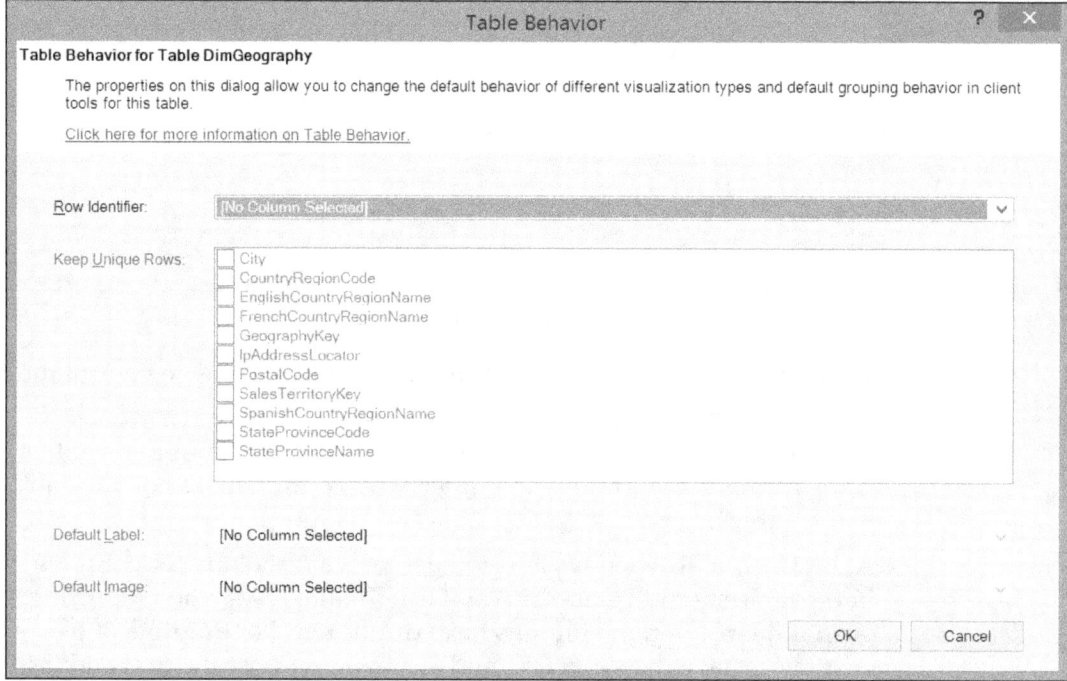

Table Behavior dialog box

- **Data Category**: This is a property setting that is accessible on any column in your data model. The available values for this property are **Address**, **City**, **Continent**, **Country**, **County**, **Image**, **Image URL**, **Latitude**, **Longitude**, **Organization**, **Place**, **PostalCode**, **StateOrProvince**, and **WebUrl**. Power View can interpret the value you set to improve the report. For example, if the value is set to **Image URL**, then the Power View report will display the image, or if it is set to **Country**, it will map the data. To set the data category for a data model, go to a PowerPivot window, and on the **Advanced** tab, there is a **Reporting Properties** section with the **Data Category** field (see the following screenshot). To set the data category for a tabular model, in SSDT, go to the properties of the appropriate column, and in the **Data Category** property, click on the drop-down button.

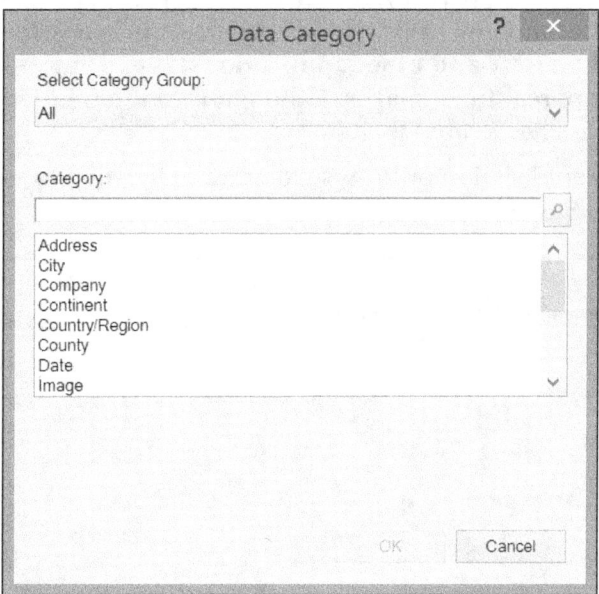

# Deploying and sharing reports

Once the Power View reports are created, it is time to deploy them so that they can be shared with others. If you create your Power View report directly in SharePoint, you can quickly and easily save the report to a PowerPivot Gallery, and it can be shared by others using following steps:

1. Once the Power View report in SharePoint is complete, select the **FILE** tab in the ribbon.
2. Click on **Save** and enter a filename for the report file, which will be given the file extension of .rdlx (see the following screenshot).
3. You have the option to save preview images of the report so that other users can see them in the PowerPivot Gallery view pane by checking the **Include an image of each view in its current state as a preview for other users (in PowerPivot Gallery and other applications)** box. They are snapshots of the report and not real-time images, although they are frequently refreshed. This option is checked by default.
4. Use the current location or browse to another location to store the report file and click on **Save**.

Saving a Power View report in SharePoint

If the Power View report is contained in an Excel workbook, you can save it to SharePoint using the same steps in the previous PowerPivot section.

# Presentation modes

A Power View report is always presentable, meaning there is no need to switch to a preview mode to see how your report looks. When using Power View in SharePoint, by default, a report is in design mode. There is also a reading mode in which the ribbon and field list are hidden and the report takes up the whole browser. This is also the case in the full-screen presentation mode (just like a PowerPoint slide show). In both modes, the **Filters Area** will be visible if it was visible in the design mode.

To switch to either mode, on the **HOME** tab, choose **Reading Mode** or **Full Screen**. To toggle between the views in either mode, use the arrow keys or click on the multi-view icon at the lower left of the screen. You can interact with the report visualizations just like you can in the design mode, but you can't edit the report.

# Reports with multiple views in Power View

When using Power View in SharePoint, you can create a single report with multiple views, where all the views in the report are based on the same data model (see the following screenshot). You can click on each view while giving a presentation, much like you can in Microsoft Office PowerPoint. You are able to copy and paste from one view to another as well as duplicate whole views. You can do something similar for Power View in Excel by creating an Excel workbook with multiple Power View sheets. So in Power View in SharePoint, a report can have multiple views, and in Power View in Excel, a report can have multiple sheets.

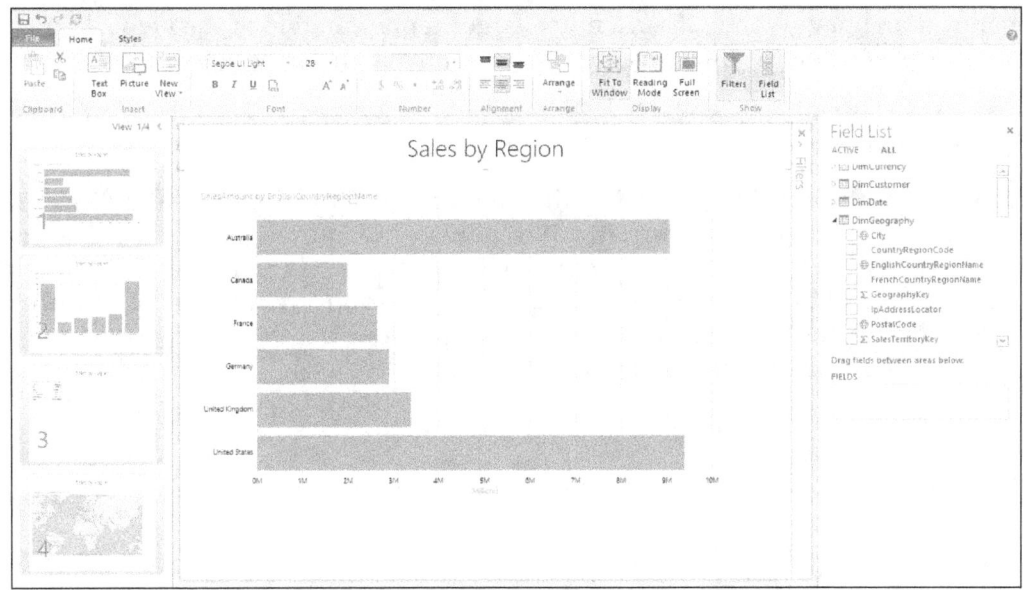

Multiple views in Power View

## Adding multiple views

To add a new view to a report, perform the following steps:

1. Open the report that you want to add the new view to.
2. On the **HOME** tab, click on **New View**, and then from the drop-down menu, select **New View**. The new view will be displayed in the left-hand side pane.

To add a duplicate view to a report, follow these steps:

1. Open the report that you want to add the duplicate view to.
2. On the **HOME** tab, click on **New View**, and from the drop-down menu, select **Duplicate View**. The duplicate view will be displayed in the left-hand side pane. This second view is the default view and is the one displayed in the canvas.

## Navigating among views

In any presentation mode (design, reading, or fullscreen), you can use the up and down arrow keys to switch to any of the views in the report. In design mode, you can click on any of the views in the left-hand side pane. In reading and fullscreen modes, in the lower left, there is a **View Chooser** button that you can use to show a row of the views in the report. This button will activate the story board view in which you will see a tab strip with images of all the views that are included in the report; the tab strip is at the bottom of the screen below the existing view. If you hover over an image, you will see a much larger representation of the view.
You can also click on the image that is on the strip, making it the active view.

## View filters

Each view has its own filter; however, the filter area is of the same size for all views. If you adjust the size for one view, it will be adjusted for all views. The filter choices for each view persist as you switch from one view to another. So if you set a filter on a view, leave, and then come back, the filter will be as you left it. When you duplicate a view, the filter and the filter choices will be duplicated too. When you save a report, the filter choices are saved too.

## View preview images

As mentioned in the *Deploy and share reports* section, if you save the preview images when saving the report, they will be displayed in the **View** pane in the design mode.

## Chart highlighting, slicers, and filtering

Power View provides different ways to filter and highlight data in reports. Since the underlying data model contains metadata, Power View knows the relationships between the various tables and fields in a report, so one visualization can be used to filter all the other visualizations. Chart highlighting, slicers, and filters are three of the ways to filter all the visualizations in a view in Power View (SharePoint) or all the visualizations in a sheet in Power View (Excel). You can choose to create filters for the whole view or sheet or for individual visualizations. None of these filters apply across the whole report: in Power View in SharePoint, they are specific to individual views in the report. In Power View in Excel, they are specific to individual sheets in the report. All of the filters allow you to select one or more values.

### Chart highlighting

Charts can act as filters via interactive cross-filtering. When you select a value by clicking directly on the chart, it will filter the values in all the tables, titles, and bubble charts in the view or sheet based on the value you clicked on. It also highlights parts of the charts that pertain to the value, showing the impact of the filtered values on the original values. You can select multiple values by using *Ctrl + left-click*. To clear a filter, click inside the background of a report item, not on a value. Interactive cross-filtering selections are saved when you move from one view or sheet to another, but are not saved with the report.

*Power View – Self-service Reporting*

In the following example, the **Professional** value is selected by clicking on it in the pie chart legend. This action results in the bar chart display the **SalesAmount** value for only the selected **EnglishOccupation** in a dark color, with the overall values in a lighter shade. Values in the two tables are also filtered by the selected **ProfessionalEnglishOccupation**.

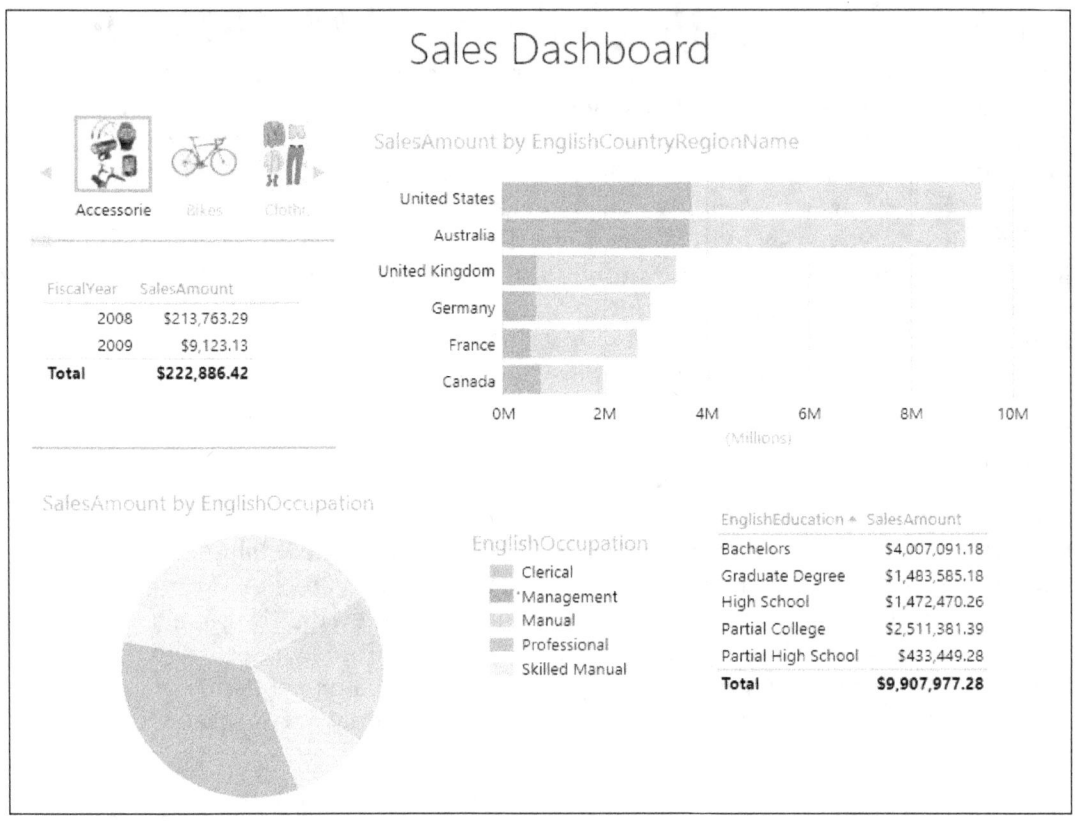

Interactive cross-filtering

# Slicers

Slicers are a type of filter and are identical to the slicers you find in Excel. They filter everything in the view or sheet. To build one, you first create a single-column table from any attribute field, select the table, and click on the **Slicer** button. Each value in the table becomes a button, and when you click on the button, the data is filtered in the report immediately. You select multiple values by holding the *Ctrl* key when you click on each button. There is a **Clear Filter** icon at the top-right of each slicer that resets the filter, resulting in all values being selected. You can then click on any value to deselect it.

Note that clicking on a value in a table that is not a slicer does *not* filter the report. You can add multiple slicers to your report (see the **Promotion Dashboard** screenshot in the *Getting started* section). Be aware that slicers filter each other. So, for example, in the **Promotion Dashboard** screenshot, we have a slicer for **FiscalYear, Gender,** and **SalesTerritoryRegion**. When you click on a fiscal year, it filters the other two slicers to show only the particular gender and sales territory regions for that fiscal year. The result is the filtering effects of all slicers are combined.

Slicers are different than chart highlighting in the following three ways:

- They filter charts rather than highlighting charts
- They are saved with the report, so when that same report is reopened, the same values in the slicer will be selected
- They allow for the use of image fields as the slicer, in which case the **Row Identifier** field for that image will be used as the filter in the slicer

In the following screenshot, the product category slicer on the left-hand side is filtered by bikes, so only the bikes in the product subcategory slicer on the right-hand side are displayed. In effect, the slicer on the left-hand side filters the values in the slicer on the right.

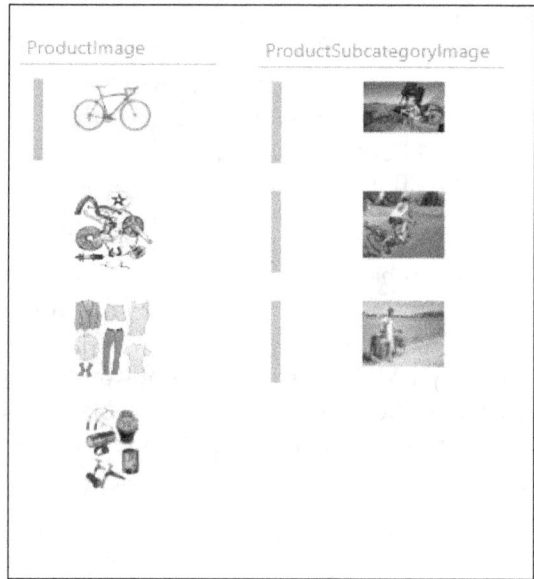

Slicers

# Filtering

Power View has basic and advanced filters that can be applied to an individual visualization or to the whole view or sheet, but not the entire report. There is a specific Filters Area for these filters that are saved with the report. If you set a filter in the Filters Area, it will continue to filter the report even if you close the Filters Area. Note that you cannot filter an image field.

## View-level/sheet-level filters

A view-level or sheet-level filter will filter all the visualizations as well as all the slicers in the view or sheet. To see the Filters Area, on the **HOME** tab, click on **Filters** in Power View in SharePoint or Filters Area in Power View in Excel. You can also click on the **Show Filters** icon in the top-right corner on any visualization. To add fields to the Filters Area, drag the fields over from the fields section of the fields list or click on the down arrow to the right-hand side of a field in the field section of the fields list and click on **Add to View Filter**.

## Visualization-level filters

You can create a filter that will be applied to only one visualization. This visualization can be a table, matrix, card, or chart, but not a slicer or tile container. If you wish to view the filters on a visualization, click on the **Show Filters** icon in the top-right corner of the visualization. The fields in the visualization will then be displayed in the **Filters** area so that you able to filter them. You can drag other fields from the fields list to the **Filters** area; this can be done even for fields that are not part of that visualization. Alternatively, you can click on the down arrow to the right-hand side of a field in the field section of the fields list and click on **Add to <visualization type> Filter**.

If you expand the **Filters** area, when you select a visualization, you will see the visualization type in a gray heading to the right-hand side of the word **VIEW** in the **Filters** area. For example, if you select a chart, you will see a **VIEW** heading and to its right-hand side, a **CHART** heading in the **Filters** area (see the following screenshot). Click on the **VIEW** heading to see the view-level/sheet-level filters and click on the **CHART** heading to see the filters for the selected chart.

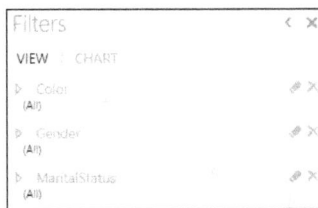

Filters area

Any filter that you add to a visualization can be deleted using the **Delete filter** icon, located to the right-hand side of the filter name (see the previous screenshot). However, you cannot delete the filters for any field that are in the visualization. Rather, you can clear them so that they have no effect. Note that if you add a filter for a field that is in the visualization and later delete that field from the visualization, the filter will remain in effect for that visualization. To remove the filter, you will need to go to the **Filters** area for that particular visualization and delete the filter.

## Basic filters

In the **Filters** area, by default, you will use basic filters. Click on the right-arrow to the left of any filter name to expand the filter (see the following screenshot). For non-numeric basic filters, there will be checkboxes for each value that you can select and deselect. There will be a number after each value that indicates how many records have that value. For numeric basic filters, there will be a slider that you can drag to select the values between the markers.

Expanded filter

## Advanced filters

You can use advanced filters by selecting the **Advanced filter mode** icon to the right-hand side of each field filter. This will open up an advanced filter dialog as shown in the following screenshot:

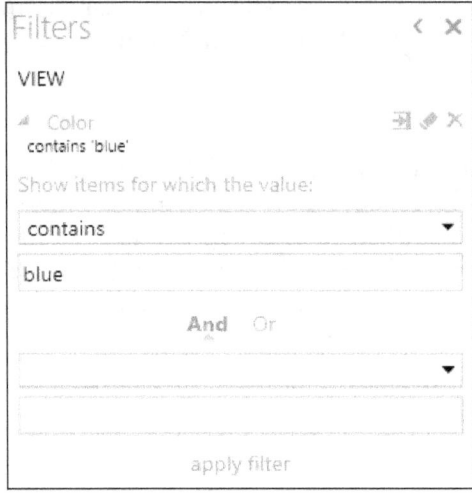

Advanced filter

With this option you can apply multiple filters using **And/Or**. Each filter can be a range of values or freeform values. You can enter partial values to be included or excluded. There is a drop-down list of phrases to choose from as shown in the following screenshot:

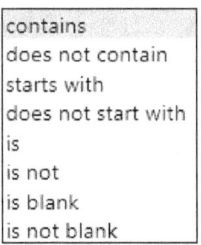

Advanced filter phrases

## Search in filters

When you expand a filter, you will see a search box (see the earlier **Expanded filter** screenshot). This will allow you to search for a value in a text field within a visualization or view level (it does not search the whole report). You can then choose whether to filter on it. The portion of a field's value that matches the search text is highlighted in yellow in the search result list. You can use wildcard characters in the search box: a question mark (?) will match any single character and an asterisk (*) will match any sequence of characters. Use the tilde (~) before the question mark or asterisk if you actually want to find a question mark or asterisk. A search is not case-sensitive.

For example, in a list of colors, typing l*e in the search box returns three colors: **blue**, **silver**, and **silver/black**.

## Sorting

In Power View, you can sort data in tables, bar and columns charts, and matrices. You can also sort measures and nonmeasures.

To sort tables and matrices, click on the column heading you want sorted. You will then see an up arrow, indicating the field is sorted in ascending order, or a down arrow, indicating the field is sorted in descending order. Click on the column heading again to change the sort criteria. With flat tables, you can only sort one column at a time. With matrices, you can sort the whole matrix in one measure column or sort one nonmeasure column in each grouping level.

With charts, by default, they are sorted alphabetically in ascending order by the first chart category (unless a sort order is specified in the data model). You can sort chart categories by a category value in the **Axis** box or by a measure value in the **Values** box. Note that line, scatter, or bubble charts cannot be sorted.

If your visualization is made up of images only, Power View will sort by the **Sort by Other Column** property. If not, and the data model has a **Default Label** column, it will sort that column. If neither, it will sort on the **Row ID** field.

# Export reports to Microsoft Office PowerPoint

There is another cool feature that you can use with Power View reports created in SharePoint: you can export the reports to PowerPoint (note that this does not work with reports created in Excel). When exporting, each view in Power View becomes a separate Silverlight control in its own PowerPoint slide. To export and view within PowerPoint, follow these steps:

1. Save the Power View report as you can't export an unsaved report.
2. Click on **Export to PowerPoint** in the **File** menu (see the following screenshot).
3. Save the new PowerPoint presentation.
4. Open the saved presentation in PowerPoint. You will see a static image of each view in Power View that is centered on a separate slide.
5. At the lower-right corner of PowerPoint, click on **Reading View** or **Slide Show**.
6. In the lower-right corner of the PowerPoint slide, click to load the live Power View report from the SharePoint server. You can then interact with it.

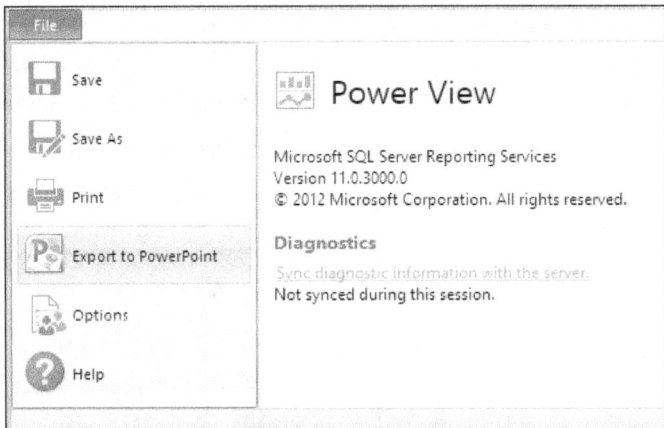

Exporting to PowerPoint

The PowerPoint presentation will be an interactive report, not just a static snapshot, as long as it can access the Power View report on the SharePoint server. This means you can filter and slice and dice the report. When you update and save the Power View report in SharePoint, the next time you view the PowerPoint slide, you will see the updates to the Power View report. Exporting to PowerPoint requires the **Open Items** SharePoint permission.

Another benefit of exporting reports to PowerPoint is that it allows you to print all of the reports at the same time (in SharePoint, you can only print one view at a time within a report file). Also, once exported to PowerPoint, you can save the reports to PDF format, since there is no way to export to PDF while in SharePoint.

## Design tips

The following are descriptions of some features and tips that make it easier to create reports in Power View in Excel and in SharePoint.

## Undo/Redo

Almost anything you do when designing a report can be undone using the **Undo** button. This allows you to experiment with any feature to learn about it, and if you don't like it, just use **Undo**. You are able to undo multiple steps in the order in which you did them, and if you undo too many times, you can use the **Redo** button. In Power View in Excel, the **Undo** and **Redo** buttons are the large forward and backward arrows that are on the **Power View** tab. In Power View in SharePoint, they are two small buttons at the top left-hand side, separate from the tabs.

## Arranging visualizations

When populating a report with multiple visualizations, one item can overlap or completely cover another, for example, you could place a smaller graph on top of a larger graph. To provide flexibility in the design, you can bring objects forward or all the way to the front, or move objects backward or all the way to the back. In Power View in Excel, this is accomplished by the **Bring Forward** and **Send Backward** buttons in the **Arrange** section in the **Design** tab. In Power View in SharePoint, use the **Arrange** button in the **Home** tab.

## Fit to window

The Power View report in Microsoft Excel as well as in SharePoint fits to the window and automatically resizes if you open more panes, such as the **Filters** area, or if you resize the window, it resizes by adjusting the font size of all the objects. To stop the report from resizing to fit the window, click on the **Fit to Window** button. Then, if the report is too big to fit the canvas area, use the scroll bars to view the different parts of the report.

## Pop out

Every visualization has a **Pop out** icon in the upper-right corner. Clicking on this will expand the visualization to fill the entire Power View window (or the entire mode if you are in the reading or fullscreen mode). It will cover all the other visualizations, but clicking on the **Pop out** icon again (which will now say **Pop in**), will return the report to its previous state. Note that tiles do not have a **Pop out** icon.

## Summary

In this chapter, we learned about the features of Power View and how it is an excellent tool for self-service reporting. We talked about PowerPivot and BISM and how they relate to Power View. We covered setting up and using Power View within SharePoint and how to connect to a tabular model as well as a multidimensional model. Then, we talked about using Power View within Excel via data models and how to import data into Excel. We moved on to data visualizations, describing the different types of reports you can create. We covered the Power View user interface and how to enhance the data models. We discussed how to deploy and share reports, the various presentation modes, and reports with multiple views. A large section was on chart highlighting, slicers, and filters. We ended with a discussion on sorting, exporting to PowerPoint, and design tips. In the next chapter, we will show you step-by-step how to create a report in Power View.

# 5
# Development Activity with Power View

In this chapter, we'll walk through the process of creating a basic **Power View** report. As we learned in the previous chapter, Power View reports can be created using Excel 2013 or directly through the browser when connected to a SharePoint site, which has the **Reporting Services Add-in for SharePoint Products** installed. In the following development activity, we will be leveraging the second option.

The development activity in this chapter is broken up into the following sections:

- Creating a BI Semantic Model (BISM) connection
- Opening the Power View design interface
- Creating bar charts
- Creating pie charts
- Creating column charts
- Adding a slicer
- Deploying reports to SharePoint

## Prerequisites

Before you start this exercise, you will require the following:

- Access to a server running SharePoint Server 2010 Enterprise Edition or SharePoint Server 2013 with the Reporting Services Add-in for SharePoint Products installed

- Access to a Microsoft SQL Server 2012 Analysis Services instance installed in tabular mode with the Adventure Works 2012 sample tabular database deployed
- A browser with Microsoft Silverlight 5 installed

Microsoft SharePoint Server 2013 is available in a 180-day trial version from the following location: `http://technet.microsoft.com/en-us/evalcenter/hh973397.aspx`

Microsoft SQL Server 2012 is available in a 180-day trial version (which includes SQL Server Data Tools) from the following location: `http://www.microsoft.com/en-us/download/details.aspx?id=29066`

Adventure Works DW 2012 sample database is available for download from the following location: `http://msftdbprodsamples.codeplex.com/releases/view/55330`

## Tutorial scenario

In this exercise, you will step into the shoes of a business user working in the sales department at a fictitious bike retailer called Adventure Works. You have been tasked with creating a report for the department that will provide a breakdown of internet sales by customer attributes, product categories, and geography. After developing the report, you will need to deploy it to the company's existing SharePoint site where it can be accessed by other users in the sales department.

## Creating a BI Semantic Model (BISM) connection

Before Power View reports can be created in SharePoint, a connection object must be created pointing to the data source, which in this demo will be an Analysis Services Tabular model. This task is typically carried out by IT ahead of time since it usually requires a bit more technical knowledge about the systems' infrastructure than can be reasonably expected of the business users.

However, for the sake of this exercise, we will quickly walk through the process of creating BISM connection file, which as you learned in the previous chapter, is only one of the methods for connecting to a tabular model from Power View in SharePoint.

 The following link contains detailed information with regards to creating BI Semantic Model (BISM) connection objects pointing to Analysis Services Tabular models: http://technet.microsoft.com/en-us/library/hh230972.aspx

Follow these steps:

1. Open a browser and navigate to the **Data Connections** library in which you wish to create the BISM connection file.
2. Select **BI Semantic Model Connection** from the **New Document** dropdown as shown in the following screenshot:

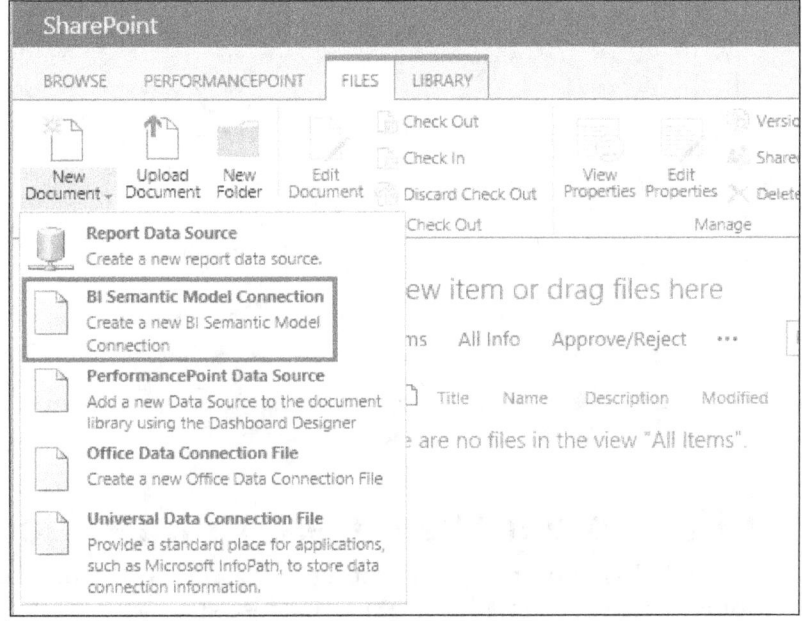

New Document drop-down menu to create BI Semantic Model Connection

On the **New BI Semantic Model Connection** page, fill in the values specific to your environment and click on **OK** to create the BISM connection file. Use the following screenshot for guidance, but keep in mind that the values for the last two fields are specific to my environment. If you are not sure what values to supply for your environments, review the instructions under the **Connection Information** section at the bottom of the **New BI Semantic Model Connection** page to determine the appropriate values for your environment.

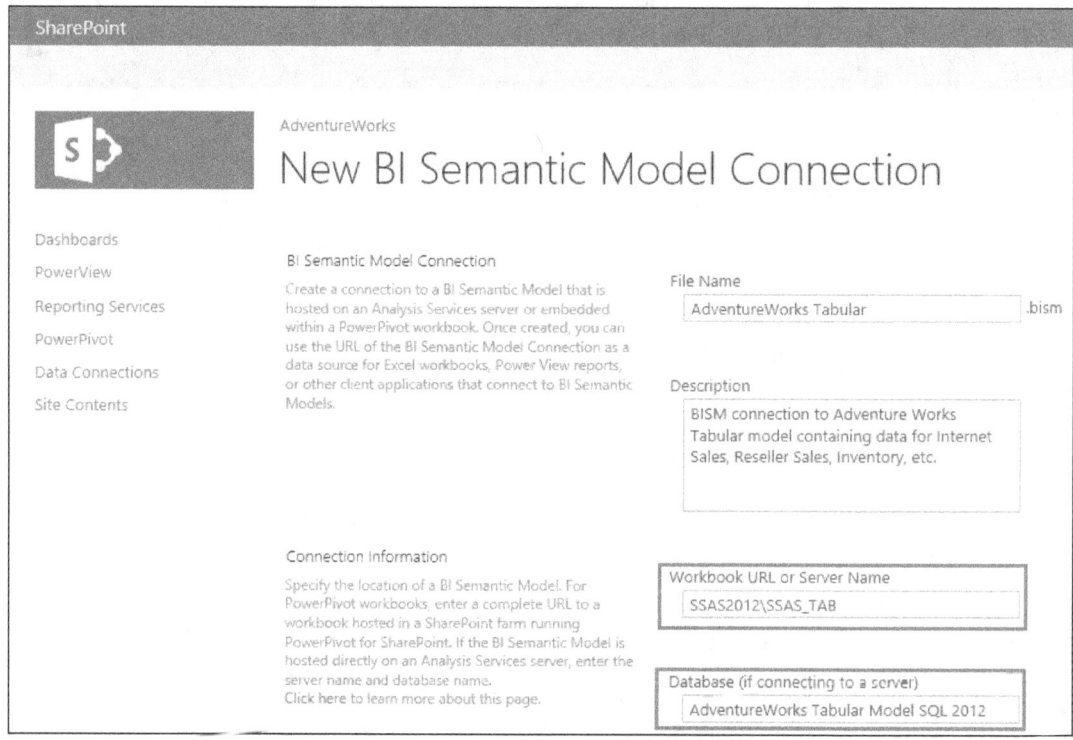

New BI Semantic Model Connection page

# Opening the Power View design interface

Now that we have a BISM connection file pointing to the tabular model, we are ready to begin developing the Power View report. Follow these steps:

1. Click on the name of the BISM connection file created in the previous section to open the Power View report design interface.

2. Click on the textbox at the top of the canvas labeled **Click here to add a title**, and enter `Sales Report`. Your screen should resemble the one in the following screenshot:

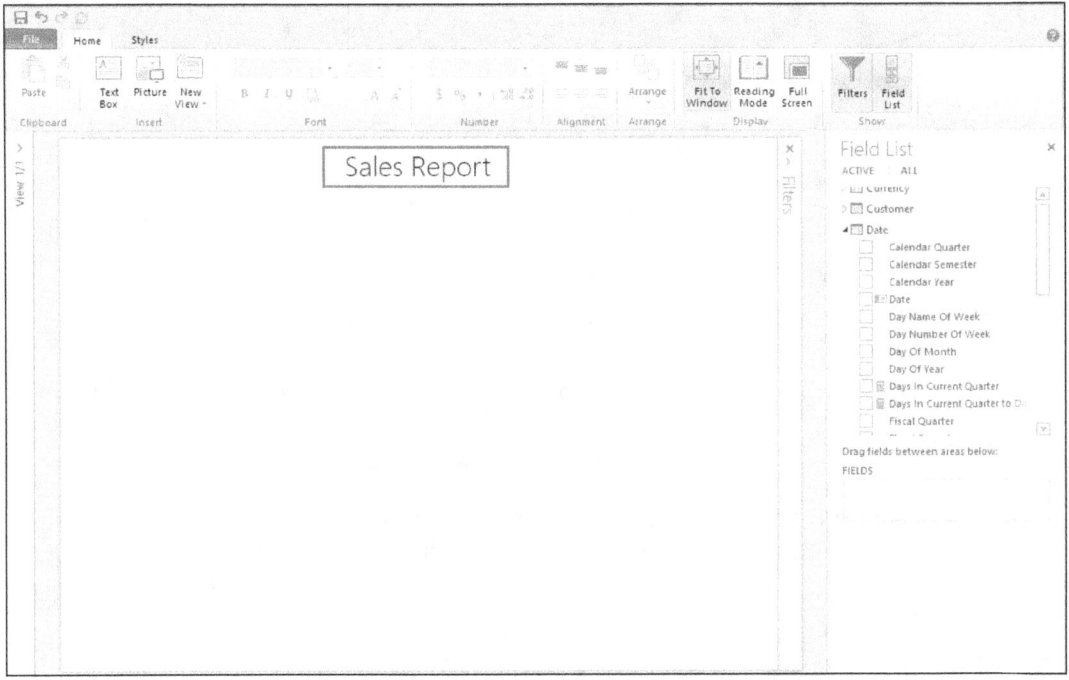

Power View design interface after adding the report title

## Creating bar charts

The first object we will add to the Power View report is a bar chart comparing `Sales Amount` by `Country`. Follow these steps:

1. Click on a blank space on the canvas.
2. In the **Field List**, locate and expand the `Internet Sales` table.
3. Click on the checkbox next to the field labeled `Sales Amount` as shown in the following screenshot:

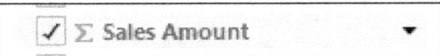

4. Now locate and expand the Geography table in the field list, and click on the checkbox next to the Country Region Name field, as shown in the following screenshot:

Field list in Power View design interface

5. At this point, the report body contains a table showing Sales Amount by Country Region Name and should resemble the following screenshot:

Report body with table showing Sales Amount by Country Region Name

6. In the visualizations group of the ribbon, click on the **Bar** button to convert the table into a horizontal bar chart.
7. Now increase the size of the bar chart object by clicking on the bottom-right corner of the bar chart and dragging it out towards the bottom-right corner of the screen, as in the following screenshot:

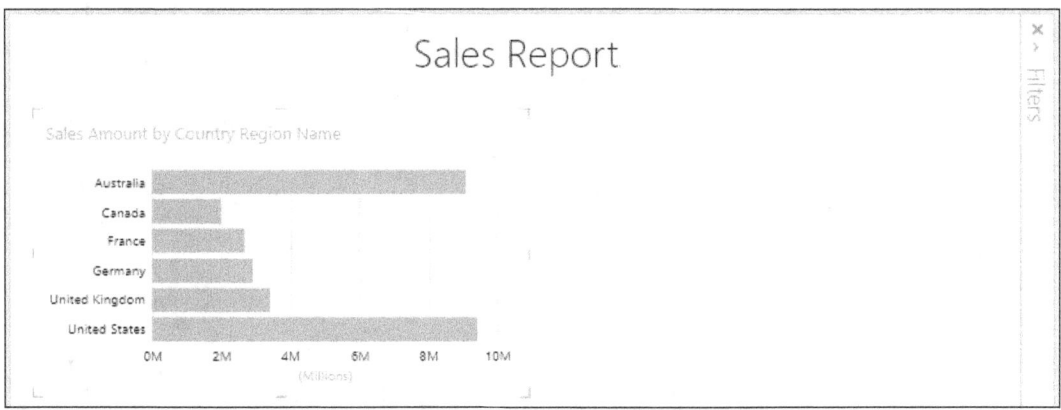

Bar chart visualization of Sales Amount by Country Region Name

# Creating pie charts

The next object that we will add to the Power View report is a pie chart comparing `Sales Amount` by `Customer Occupation` by following these steps:

1. Click on a blank space on the canvas.
2. In the **Field List**, locate and expand the `Internet Sales` table.
3. Click on the checkbox next to the `Sales Amount` field.
4. Move the object to the upper-right corner of the canvas in to the right of the bar chart.
5. Now locate and expand the `Customer` table in the field list and click on the checkbox next to `Occupation`.

6. With the new object still in focus, click on the drop-down button in the visualizations group of the ribbon (shown in the following screenshot), and select the **Pie** button.

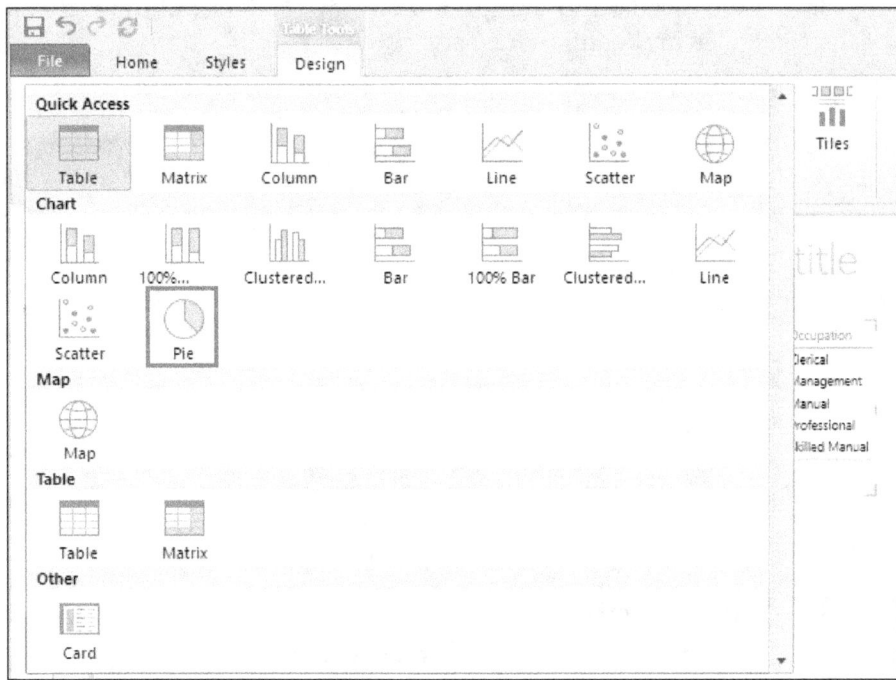

7. Just as with the bar chart in the previous section, click on and hold the bottom-right corner of the pie chart object and drag it out towards the bottom-right corner of the screen to increase the size. Your report canvas should now resemble the following screenshot:

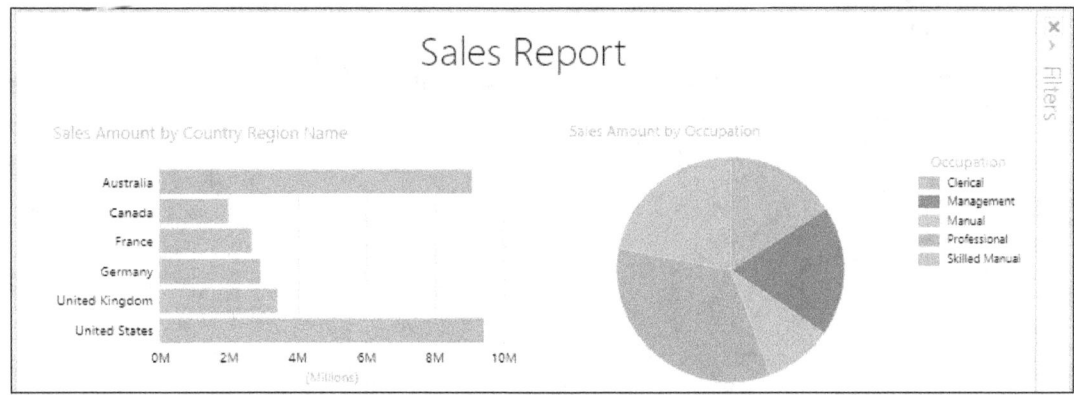

Bar chart and pie chart side by side

## Creating column charts

The next object we will add to the Power View report is a column chart comparing `Sales Amount` by `Customer Commute Distance`. Follow these steps:

1. Click on a blank space on the canvas.
2. In the **Field List**, locate and expand the `Internet Sales` table.
3. Click the checkbox next to the `Sales Amount` field.
4. Move the object to the lower-left corner of the canvas—just below the bar chart.
5. Now locate and expand the `Customer` table in the **Field List**, and click on the checkbox next to `Commute Distance`.
6. With the new object still in focus, click on the **Column** button in the visualizations group of the ribbon.
7. Just as with the bar chart and pie chart from the previous sections, click on, and hold the bottom-right corner of the column chart object and drag it out towards the bottom-right corner of the screen to increase the size. Your report canvas should now resemble the following screenshot:

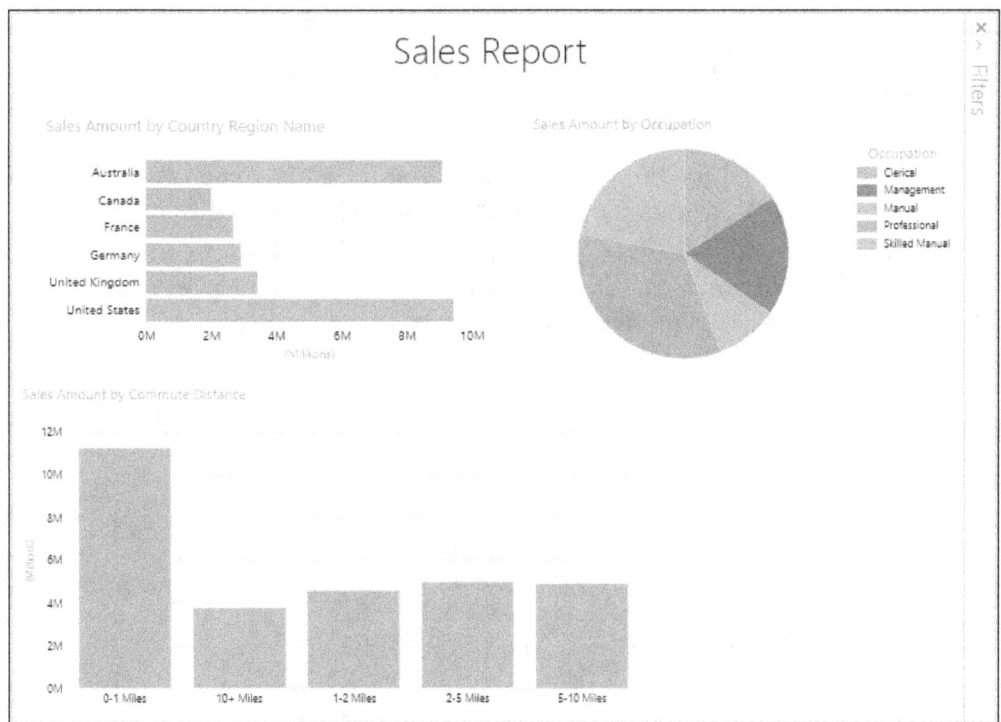

Column chart added to bottom-left corner of report body

*Development Activity with Power View*

# Adding a slicer

Now that we have a few visualizations placed on the screen, let's add a slicer object to improve user experience by providing the ability to filter the data by `Calendar Year`. Follow these steps:

1. Click on a blank space on the canvas.
2. In the **Field List**, expand the `Date` table and click on the checkbox next to `Calendar Year`.
3. Move the table of year values to the bottom-right corner of the screen.
4. Up in the ribbon, click on the **Slicer** button to convert the table of year values into a slicer object as shown in the following screenshot:

Slicer button in the ribbon

5. Click on and hold the bottom-right corner of the slicer object and drag it out towards the bottom-right corner of the screen to increase the size.
6. Now again from the ribbon, click on the button shown in the following screenshot to increase the size of the slicer values. Your report canvas should now resemble the following screenshot:

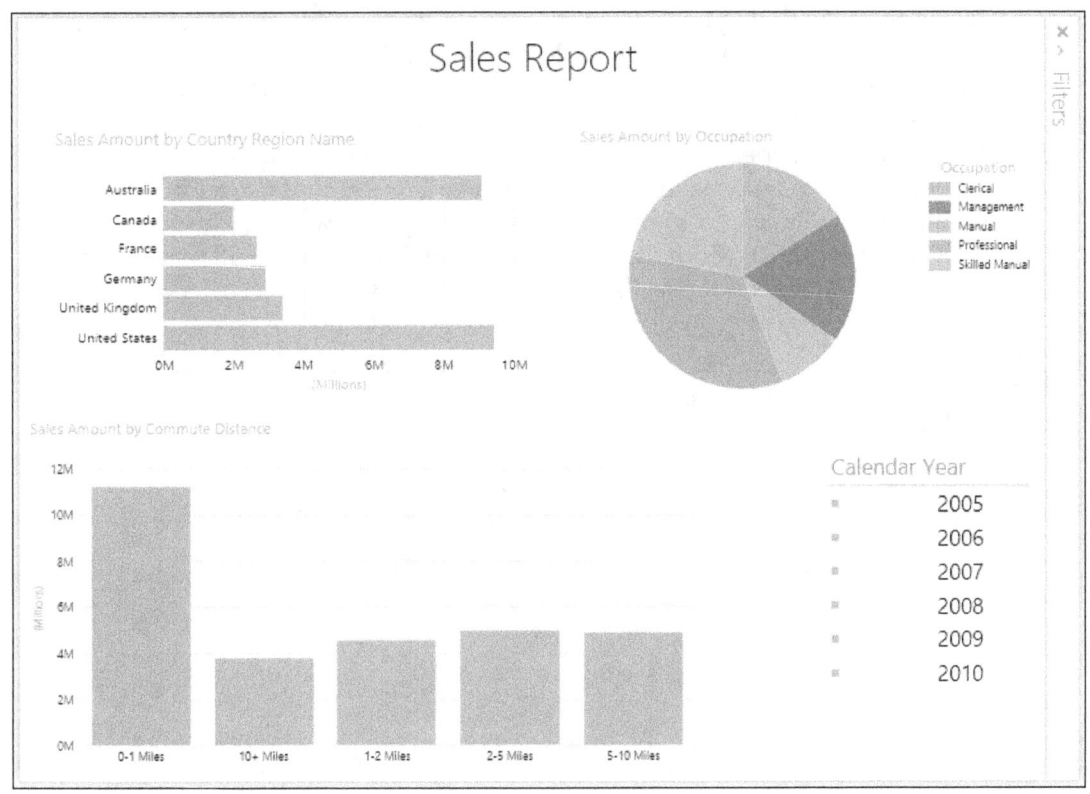

The Calendar Year slicer added to bottom-right corner of the report body

# Deploying reports to SharePoint

After spending some time testing out user experience by clicking around the report, it is time to deploy the report to SharePoint so that other users in your department can use it. Since we created this report via SharePoint, this process is really easy. Follow these steps:

1. Click on the **File** button in the upper-left corner of the ribbon and choose the **Save As** option.

*Development Activity with Power View*

2. In the **Save As** dialog box, navigate to the document library in which you wish to save the report, give the file a name, and click on the **Save** button. In the following screenshot, the report has been named Sales Report and will be saved in a document library called PowerView. This document library happens to be a special type of document library known as a PowerPivot Gallery. As you will see in the last screenshot of the chapter, a PowerPivot Gallery uses Silverlight to provide thumbnail previews of each view in a Power View report. More information on the PowerPivot Gallery document library is available at the following address: http://msdn.microsoft.com/en-us/library/ee637430.aspx

The Save As dialogue box to save a Power View report

Now other users in the sales department can access the Power View report by navigating to the document library where the report was saved.

The following screenshot shows what the rest of the users see when they navigate to the SharePoint document library where the report was saved. To run the report, the user can simply click on the thumbnail of the report.

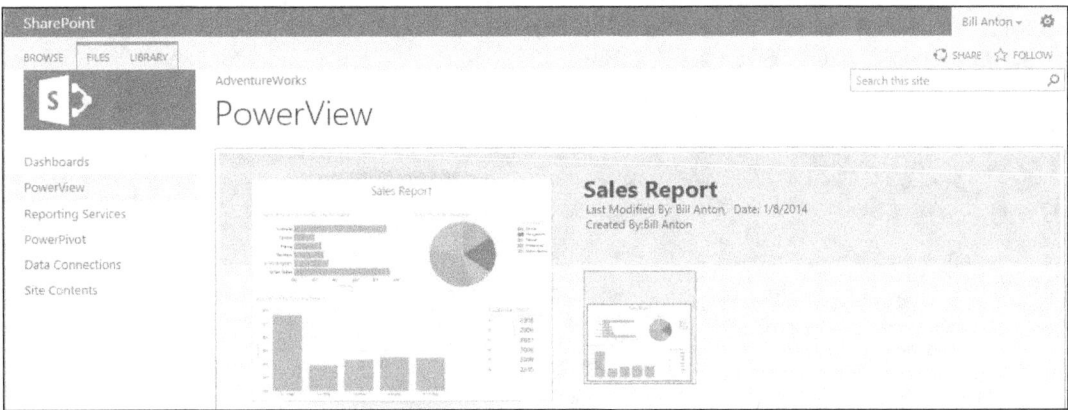

Power View report in (PowerPivot Gallery) document library

# Summary

In this chapter, we stepped into the shoes of a business user in the sales department and created a self-service report using the browser-based Power View development interface available through the SharePoint environment. The end result was a visually appealing and highly interactive report, which we created from start to finish without the need to involve IT resources. Finally, we deployed the report to a SharePoint PowerPivot Gallery (document library), where the rest of our department was now able to access the report.

# Index

## Symbols

100% Stacked Bar Chart  83
100% Stacked Column Chart  84

## A

actions
  about  32
  configuring  32
  custom code  33
  Go to bookmark type  33
  Go to report type  33
  Go to URL type  33
Advanced filter mode icon  100
advanced filters  100
Allow blank value (") parameter  29
Allow multiple values parameter  30
Allow null value parameter  29
Arrange button  103
Axis Options tab  65

## B

Bar button  111
bar charts
  creating  109-111
basic filters  99
BI Semantic Model. *See* BISM
BI Semantic Model Connection  107
BISM  73, 107
BISM connection
  creating  106, 107
Browser role  49

## C

caching
  about  42
  cache refresh plan, refreshing  43
  URL  43
canned reports  5
Canvas  87
Card  83
Category Group Properties option  62
chart highlighting  95
Chart Properties window  65
chart, report parts items  24
charts
  bar charts, creating  109-111
  column charts, creating  113
  pie charts, creating  111, 112
Clear Filter icon  96
Clustered Bar Chart  83
Clustered Column Chart  84
column charts
  creating  113
Country Region Name field  110
Credentials tab  58
custom code
  embedded  33
  external  33

## D

dashboard
  creating  13
data
  adding, to worksheet  81

adding to worksheet, PowerPivot used 82
inserting, to Power View 81
not adding, to worksheet 81
not adding to worksheet, PowerPivot used 82

**Data Alert Manager page** 45
**data alerts**
  about 43, 44
  primary components 44
  working 45
**data bar, report parts items** 26
**Data Category enhancement** 91
**data-driven subscriptions** 11, 39
**data feed** 48
**data, importing into Excel**
  adding, to worksheet 81
  adding to worksheet, PowerPivot used 82
  not adding, to worksheet 81
  not adding to worksheet, PowerPivot used 82, 83
**data models**
  enhancing 88
**dataset**
  about 18, 19
  creating 19, 59, 60
  filtering 21
  queries, entering manually 19
**data source**
  about 16, 17
  embedded 17
  list 16
  shared 17
**Data type parameter** 29
**data visualizations**
  100% Stacked Bar Chart 83
  100% Stacked Column Chart 84
  Card 83
  Clustered Bar Chart 83
  Clustered Column Chart 84
  Line Chart 84
  Map 84
  Matrix 83
  Multiples 84
  Pie Chart 84
  Scatter Chart 84
  Stacked Bar Chart 83
  Stacked Column Chart 83
  table 83
  Tiles 84
**Default Field Set enhancement** 88
**delivery option, subscription**
  Email option 38
  Network File Share option 38
  Null Delivery Provider option 39
  SharePoint Document option 38
**department solution** 74
**Design tab** 103
**development activity, with Power View**
  prerequisites 105, 106
**development activity, with SSRS**
  prerequisites 53, 54

# E

**embedded custom code** 33
**embedded data source**
  about 17
  benefits 18
**enhancements, data models**
  Data Category 91
  Default Field Set 88
  Table Behavior 89, 90
**enterprise solution** 74
**expression**
  about 31
  effects 32
**external custom code** 34

# F

**Field List** 87
**Field Well** 88
**filtering**
  about 98
  advanced filters 100
  basic filters 99
  search in filters 101
  view-level/sheet-level filters 98
  visualization-level filters 98
**Filters Area** 88
**Finance folder** 51
**Fit to Window button** 103

## G

Gauge, report parts items  25
Go to bookmark action  33
Go to report action  33
Go to URL action  33

## H

Home ribbon  86
Home tab  103

## I

image, report parts items  23
indicator, report parts items  27, 28

## K

Key Performance Indicators (KPIs)  25, 26
KPI metric measures
  Status  26
  Target  26
  Trend  26
  Value  26

## L

Layout ribbon  86
Line Chart  84
line, report parts items  22
linked report  47
list, report parts items  23

## M

map, report parts items  26
Matrix  83
matrix, report parts items  22
Microsoft Office PowerPoint
  reports, exporting to  102
Microsoft SharePoint Server 2013
  URL  106
Microsoft SQL Server 2012  54
monthly management reports
  creating  14
multidimensional model connection  78
multiples  84

multiple views report, in Power View
  about  93
  duplicate view, adding  94
  filter, viewing  94
  navigating among  94
  new view, adding  94
  preview images, viewing  95
My Reports
  about  46
  enabling  46, 47

## N

Name parameter  29
Native mode
  about  7, 35
  differentiating, with SharePoint Integrated
    mode  35
  URL  49
Number tab  64

## O

offline format  48
online format  47
Open Items SharePoint permission  102
operational reports  5
OverwriteDatasets property  66
OverwriteDataSources property  67

## P

pie charts
  about  84
  creating  111, 112
Pop out icon  104
PowerPivot  72
PowerPivot workbook
  publishing, to SharePoint  72, 73
Power View
  about  8, 70
  chart highlighting  95
  features  9
  filtering  95
  limitations  9, 10
  multiple views reports  93
  report example  71

self-service reporting 8, 9
slicers 95
through Excel 85, 86
through SharePoint 85
used, for development activity 105, 106
within Excel 2013 79
within SharePoint 74
**Power View design interface**
opening 108
**Power View, within Excel 2013**
data, importing into Excel 80
data models 79, 80
setup 79
starting with 80
**Power View, within SharePoint**
multidimensional model connected Power View, starting 78
multidimensional model connection 78
setup 74, 75
tabular model connected Power View, starting 77
tabular model connection 75, 76
**presentation modes**
switching to 93
**Preview tab 65**
**primary components, data alerts**
Alert name 44
email settings 45
Report data name 44
Rule 45
schedule settings 45
**primary components, SSRS report**
dataset 16, 18
data source 16
report item 16, 21
**Processing Options screen 40**
**Prompt parameter 29**

# Q

Query textbox 60

# R

rectangle, report parts items 23
Redo button 103
reference
adding , to shared data source 58

report
actions 32
creating, in Power View 8
deploying 92
deploying, to SharePoint 115-117
exporting, benefit 103
exporting, to Microsoft Office PowerPoint 102
expressions 31, 32
integrating, with custom applications 13
parameters 28
rendering 7
scheduling via 7
sharing 92
snapshots 39-41
**Report Builder 34**
**Report Builder 3.0 6**
**Report Data window 59**
**Report Definition Language (RDL) 6**
**report delivery options**
email 38
network File Share 38
Null Delivery Provider 39
SharePoint Document 38
**report design, creating in Power View**
Fit to Window button 103
Pop out icon 104
Redo button 103
Undo button 103
visualizations, arranging 103
**Report Designer 34**
**report development environment**
tools 34, 35
**reporting scenarios 10-13**
**Reporting Services project**
creating 54
**Reporting Services reports**
consuming 47
**Reporting Services reports, consuming ways**
data feed 48
extensibility 48
offline 48
online 47
security 49
**report item**
about 22
adding 61-65

report object
  creating 55
report parameter
  Allow blank value (") 29
  Allow multiple values 30
  Allow null value 29
  Data type 29
  general page 29
  Name 29
  Prompt 29
  Select parameter visibility 30
report parts items
  about 21
  chart 24
  data bar 26
  Gauge 25, 26
  image 23
  indicator 27, 28
  Line 22
  list 23
  map 26
  matrix 22
  rectangle 23
  Sparkline 27
  subreport 23
  table 22
  textbox 22
report project
  deploying 66, 67
Report Project Property Pages window 66
Report Properties window 34
ribbon 87

# S

Scatter Chart 84
schedules, SSRS
  caching 37, 42, 43
  snapshots 39
  Snapshots 37
  subscriptions 37
  Subscriptions 37
scheduling
  about 36
  requirement 36
search in filters 101

security
  about 49
  data security 51
  permissions 49
  Report Server objects, securing 50, 51
  roles 49
Select parameter visibility parameter 30
self-service reporting 69
self-service solution 74
shared data source
  about 17
  benefits 18
  creating 56, 57
  reference, adding to 58
SharePoint
  report, deploying to 115, 116
SharePoint Integrated mode
  about 7, 35
  differentiating, with Native mode 36
  URL 49
Show Axis Title option 63
Show Filters icon 98
simple report
  creating 11
Slicer button 114
slicers
  about 96
  adding 114
  comparing, with chart highlighting 97
snapshot
  about 40
  creating 41
  enabling 40
  purpose 39
  using 41
Solution Explorer window 66, 67
Sort by Other Column property 101
Sorting tab 63
sparkliner report parts items 27
SQL Server Analysis Services. *See* SSAS
SQL Server Data Tools for Business
      Intelligence (SSDT-BI) 6
SQL Server Data Tools (SSDT) 53, 73
SQL Server Management Studio (SSMS) 46
SQL Server Reporting Services. *See* SSRS

**SSAS**
  about 9, 73
  creating 9
**SSRS**
  about 5-7, 15, 35
  capabilities 15
  in design mode, Visual Studio 2012 used 6
  Native mode 7
  SharePoint Integrated mode 7
  used, for development activity 53, 54
  used, for standard reporting 5-7
**SSRS report**
  primary components 16
**SSRS report output**
  Report Manager 7
**Stacked Bar Chart** 83
**Stacked Column Chart** 83
**standard reporting**
  SSRS, using 6, 7
**subreport, report parts items** 23
**subscription**
  about 10, 37
  data-driven 39
  example 38
  report delivery options 38
  standard 39

# T

**Table** 83
**Table Behavior enhancement** 89
**table, report parts items** 22
**tables**
  sorting 101
**tablix** 22

**TargetDatasetFolder property** 67
**TargetDataSourceFolder property** 67
**TargetReportFolder property** 67
**TargetReportPartFolder property** 67
**TargetServerURL property** 67
**TargetServerVersion property** 67
**Test Connection button** 57
**textbox, report parts items** 22
**Tiles** 84

# U

**Undo button** 103
**user interface**
  about 84-87
  Canvas 87
  Field List 87
  Field Well 88
  Filters Area 88
  ribbon 87
  View Area 87
**USERNAME() function** 51
**User!UserId function** 52

# V

**view-level/sheet-level filters** 98
**View Area** 87
**visualization-level filters** 98

# W

**Windows Authentication option** 51
**What You See Is What You Get (WYSIWYG)** 9, 70

## Thank you for buying
## Reporting with Microsoft SQL Server 2012

## About Packt Publishing

Packt, pronounced 'packed', published its first book "Mastering phpMyAdmin for Effective MySQL Management" in April 2004 and subsequently continued to specialize in publishing highly focused books on specific technologies and solutions.

Our books and publications share the experiences of your fellow IT professionals in adapting and customizing today's systems, applications, and frameworks. Our solution based books give you the knowledge and power to customize the software and technologies you're using to get the job done. Packt books are more specific and less general than the IT books you have seen in the past. Our unique business model allows us to bring you more focused information, giving you more of what you need to know, and less of what you don't.

Packt is a modern, yet unique publishing company, which focuses on producing quality, cutting-edge books for communities of developers, administrators, and newbies alike. For more information, please visit our website: www.packtpub.com.

## About Packt Enterprise

In 2010, Packt launched two new brands, Packt Enterprise and Packt Open Source, in order to continue its focus on specialization. This book is part of the Packt Enterprise brand, home to books published on enterprise software – software created by major vendors, including (but not limited to) IBM, Microsoft and Oracle, often for use in other corporations. Its titles will offer information relevant to a range of users of this software, including administrators, developers, architects, and end users.

## Writing for Packt

We welcome all inquiries from people who are interested in authoring. Book proposals should be sent to author@packtpub.com. If your book idea is still at an early stage and you would like to discuss it first before writing a formal book proposal, contact us; one of our commissioning editors will get in touch with you.

We're not just looking for published authors; if you have strong technical skills but no writing experience, our experienced editors can help you develop a writing career, or simply get some additional reward for your expertise.

## Learning SQL Server 2008 Reporting Services

ISBN: 978-1-84719-618-7            Paperback: 512 pages

A step-by-step guide to getting the most of Microsoft SQL Server Reporting Services 2008

1. Everything you need to create and deliver data-rich reports with SQL Server 2008 Reporting Services as quickly as possible.
2. Packed with hands-on-examples to learn and improve your skills.
3. Connect and report from databases, spreadsheets, XML Data, and more.

## Learning SQL Server Reporting Services 2012

ISBN: 978-1-84968-992-2            Paperback: 566 pages

Get the most out of SQL Server Reporting Services 2012, both Native and SharePoint Integrated modes

1. Build applications using the latest Microsoft technologies: SSIS 2012, SSDT, WPF, and SharePoint 2010.
2. Reach out to the cloud and master Windows Azure Reporting Services.
3. Learn the ins and outs of SQL Server Reporting Services 2012 for Native and SharePoint Integrated modes.

Please check **www.PacktPub.com** for information on our titles

## SQL Server 2012 Reporting Services Blueprints

ISBN: 978-1-84968-508-5　　　Paperback: 246 pages

Use real-world situations to develop real-world solutions

1. Detailed coverage of the various reporting options available.
2. Build end-to-end report solutions based on SSRS.
3. Learn from realistic situations to offer outstanding solutions.

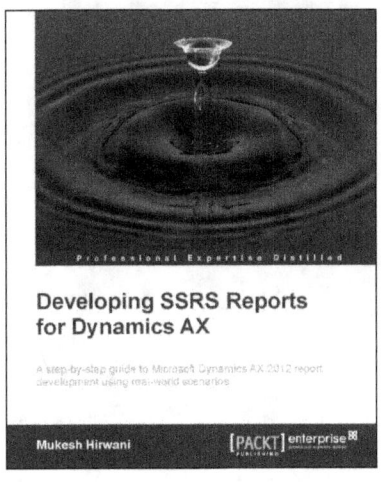

## Developing SSRS Reports for Dynamics AX

ISBN: 978-1-78217-774-6　　　Paperback: 132 pages

A step-by-step guide to Microsoft Dynamics AX 2012 report development using real-world scenarios

1. Build reports using AOT queries, report data provider classes, or an external data source.
2. Learn how to deploy reports and manage SSRS reports in AOT, as well as customize standard reports.
3. Discover best practices for Dynamics AX 2012 reporting and learn common SSRS expressions, classes, and methods.

Please check www.PacktPub.com for information on our titles

www.ingramcontent.com/pod-product-compliance
Lightning Source LLC
Chambersburg PA
CBHW062324220526
45469CB00008B/2615